EBONY PICTORIAL HISTORY OF BLACK AMERICA

EBONY PICTORIAL HISTORY OF BLACK AMERICA

By the Editors of Ebony

Introduction by
Lerone Bennett Jr.

Volume II

RECONSTRUCTION TO SUPREME COURT DECISION 1954

THE SOUTHWESTERN COMPANY, Nashville, Tennessee
By arrangement with Johnson Publishing Company, Inc., 1971

Library of Congress Catalog Card No. 71-151797

Series ISBN No. 0-87485-049-5
Volume ISBN No. 0-87485-051-7

Fourth Printing

Johnson Publishing Company, Inc.
Chicago, Illinois

Printed in the United States of America

Norman L. Hunter
Design and Layout

R.R.D. 4-72

PICTURE CREDITS

Photographs and other illustrations are identified by page number and, where necessary, by letters a, b, c, etc. in sequence on the page. Credits are listed separately for each chapter.

1

Kathleen Ann Burke, 42b
Ebony collection, 36, 37a,b, 38b,c, 39a,b,c, 40a,b,c,d, 41a,b,c, 43a,b, 59
A.S. Foley, 42a
Harpers Weekly, 2, 4, 5a,b, 6, 7, 10, 11, 12, 13, 14, 16, 18, 19, 20a,b, 23, 24, 25, 26, 28a, 29, 31, 44a,b,c, 45, 51, 52
Three Lions, Inc., 8, 30, 33, 34, 35, 47, 49

2

Amistad Research Center, New Orleans, 58b, 59a,b,c, 61b, 96b
Associated Press, 75a
Black Star, 83
Boston Guardian, 84b
Brown Brothers, 81
Ebony collection, 57b, 63, 65, 66a,b, 67, 68, 69, 71a,b, 72, 73a,b, 74a, 76, 77a,b, 78a,b, 80, 82a,b, 84a, 85, 89, 90, 91a, 92a,b,c,d,e, 93, 94a, 95a, 96a,c, 97a,b, 98a,b,c, 100, 101, 103b
Fisk University, 70
Frederick Douglass Institute, 75b
Harpers Weekly, 58a
Historical Pictures Service, Chicago, 55, 57a, 60, 61a, 86, 87a,b
NAACP, 56a,b
National Urban League, 102a,b, 103a
North Carolina Mutual Life Insurance Co., 62
Philadelphia Museum of Art, 74b
PIX Inc., 104b
Maurice Sorrell, Ebony, 64
United Press International, 94b, 104a
James Van Derzee, 95b
O.B. Willis, 91b

3

Ebony collection, 108, 109, 111, 113
Historical Pictures Service, 106
United Press International, 114

4

Ebony collection, 120, 121, 122, 123, 125, 127, 128, 130, 132, 133, 135, 137a,b, 138, 140a
Historical Pictures Service, Chicago, 140b
Underwood & Underwood, 140c
United Press International, 116, 141a,b, 142a

5

Amistad Research Center, New Orleans, 159b, 163, 177a, 184, 185, 187
Brown Brothers, 156
Chicago Defender, 194a
Joe Covelo, Black Star, 180
Detroit Free Press, 191
Ebony collection, 146, 152, 153, 159a, 160, 161, 162, 164a,b, 165a,b, 167, 170, 175a,b, 176, 177b, 182a, 190, 193, 194b
European Picture Service, 145
Ewing Galloway, 188
Mills Arts Co., 189
Antony Ostende, 178
Scolamiero Photo, 179
United Press International, 148, 154, 157, 169, 172, 174, 192
James Van Derzee, 149, 150, 151a,b, 155, 183

6

Ebony collection, 214a, 216a, 224, 225, 226b, 230, 234, 235a,b, 236a,b,c, 237b, 238a, 239a, 240a,b
European Picture Service, 233a
Historical Pictures Service, Chicago, 199, 202
David Jackson, Ebony, 226a
Jacob Ruppert, 236e
Moneta Sleet Jr., Ebony, 239b
Twentieth Century Fox, 237a
United Press International, 196, 201, 204, 206, 207, 208, 209, 210, 211, 212, 214b, 215, 218a,b, 219a,b, 220a,b, 223, 228, 229a,b, 231, 232a, 232b, 238b, 241, 242
James Van Derzee, 203, 233b
Volpe Photo, 236d
Werner Wolff, Black Star, 216b
Wide World, 227

7

Associated Press, 301, 311c,e
Chicago Sun Times, 289
Columbia Records, 294
Joe Covello, 293, 304b
Ebony collection, 248, 249, 287, 288, 290b, 297, 304a, 306, 309a,b, 310, 311a,b
Toni Frissell-PIX, Inc. 258, 259, 260
Hurok Attractions, 295a
Victor F. Kayfetz, Three Lions, Inc., 284
MGM, 291a
New York Daily News, 300b
Posie Studio, 292b
Robert Scurlock, 285
Mike Shea, 307b
Moneta Sleet Jr., Ebony, 305
Dennis Stock, 295b
George Tapscott, 308c
Twentieth Century Fox, 290a
United Artists, 291b, 292a
United Press International, 236, 250, 251, 272, 274, 276, 277a,b, 278, 279, 280, 281a,b, 282, 298, 306a, 307a, 308a,b
U.S. Army, 244, 262a,b, 264, 265, 266, 270, 271, 275a,b, 286, 303
U.S. Army Air Force, 254a, 256, 257, 302
U.S. Army Signal Corps, 254b, 255, 261, 267, 268, 269
U.S. Department of Defense, 300a
U.S. Marine Corps, 253
U.S. Navy, 247
Wide World, 299
G. Marshall Wilson, Ebony, 296

Contents

1

Reconstruction

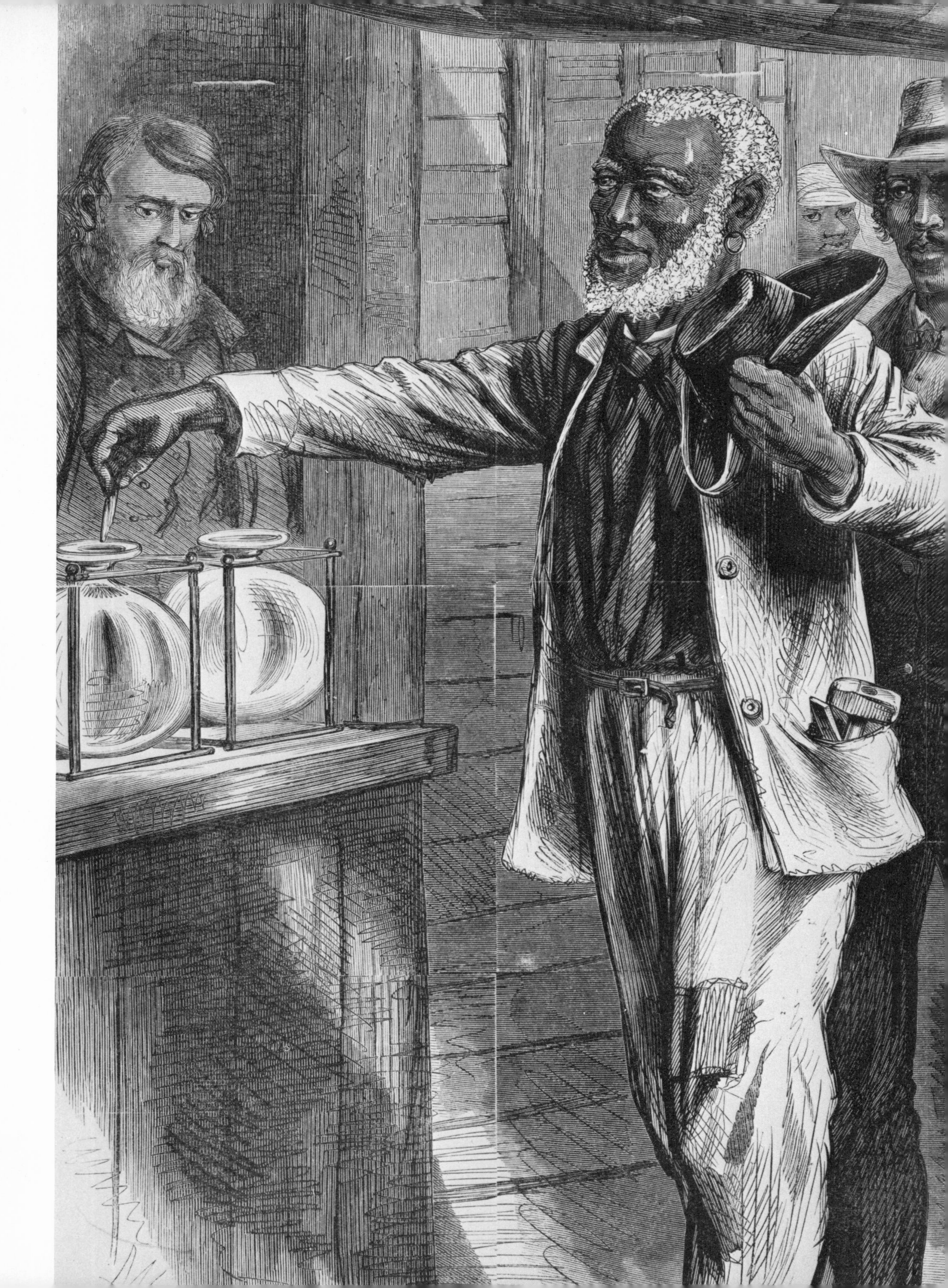

THE END of the Civil War marked the close of one era in the history of the United States and the beginning of another—one which would be racked by conflict between the president and Congress and between freedmen and their former slavemasters, but one in which blacks would assume unprecedented political power and the nation would begin thrusting toward a position of great power, of extraordinary wealth.

The war had settled two questions for all time: the United States would remain an undivided nation and blacks would no longer be slaves. The South's secessionist attempt had been crushed by superior force on the battlefield. After two hundred years of bondage, blacks could now rejoice with promises, with hope. The promises would rest forever on the national conscience; the hope would eventually be crushed.

The immediate postwar problem was the status of the South. Were Southern states still *states*, despite their four-year struggle to destroy the Union? Or had they committed acts so treasonous that they had become merely *territories* for the federal government to readmit to the Union on certain conditions?

There was another question, an enormously important one: what would be the place of the nearly four million blacks for whom freedom had been won? It was this question and the nation's response to it that would emerge as the dominant characteristic of the Reconstruction era, the first twelve postwar years (1865–77).

In the North and in Congress there

UNION
EQUAL
RIGHTS
MY FRIENDS
K.K.K.
REBELLION

The victory of the North over the South is depicted (left) in a drawing in *Harper's Weekly.*

A black village in 1866: the Trent River settlement, opposite New Bern, North Carolina.

were those who had little sympathy for the South. Many were unwilling to make concessions to rebels who had brought the nation to war and caused the expenditure of billions of dollars and the loss of hundreds of thousands of lives on both sides. But the prevailing mood of the nation after Appomattox was one of conciliation.

President Lincoln had set that mood very early in the war, saying even as the conflict raged that his attitude was one of ". . . malice toward none." He never doubted that federal forces would triumph over the dissidents, and he began formulating a plan for restoration of Confederate states. His first move would be to send in provisional military governors until civilian authority could be established again. He actually appointed such governors in 1862 for Tennessee, North Carolina, and Louisiana, and the following year, on December 8, 1863, he issued a proclamation in which the details of his blueprint were explained. He offered amnesty to all rebels (except certain high-ranking Confederate officials) who would swear future allegiance to the Union. He provided that in any Southern state (except Virginia, where he had already recognized Governor Francis H. Pierpoint's loyal government) where a minimum of 10 percent of the qualified voters in the 1860 election took the loyalty oath, a state government could be formed. As soon as that government repealed its state's acts of secession and agreed, in line with the Emancipation Proclamation, to abolish slavery, it would be recognized by the president. Because they had not voted in the 1860 election, freed slaves were to be excluded from this "political reconstruction." Actually President Lincoln did not believe in general enfranchisement of blacks.

Louisiana, Arkansas, and Tennessee began carrying out Lincoln's "10 percent plan" in late 1864 and early 1865 and actually sent representatives to Washington. But these representatives ran head on into men in Congress, "Radical Republicans" they were called, who were bitterly opposed to the president's plan. Representatives Thaddeus Stevens of Pennsylvania and Benjamin Butler of Massachusetts, and Senators Oliver Perry Morton of Indiana, Benjamin Wade of Ohio, and Charles

These drawings depict life in Trent River. Left, a schoolhouse and chapel. Right, the town's huts.

Sumner and Henry Wilson of Massachusetts—such men favored a "hard peace" for the South. They argued that Lincoln was being far too lenient, and they contended that neither the Emancipation Proclamation, which rested on the war powers of the president, nor the "10 percent plan" sufficiently guaranteed the total abolition of slavery and protected the rights of freedmen. The Radicals succeeded in getting congressional approval, in July 1864, of the Wade-Davis Bill, a measure sponsored by Senator Wade and Republican Henry Winter Davis of Maryland, which provided that, instead of Lincoln's "10 percent," a *majority* of a state's voters in the 1860 election would have to take an oath of loyalty to the Union. And there would have to be an "ironclad" oath that arms had not been borne voluntarily against the United States. Lincoln refused to sign the bill, saying it rejected "the Christian principles of forgiveness on terms of repentence." He disposed of the bill with a "pocket veto" which so angered some members of Congress that they issued a denunciation of the president. The Wade-Davis Manifesto condemned Lin-

Drawing (left) depicts the role of the Freedmen's Bureau. Bureau officials meet (above) with blacks.

coln's actions and declared that Congress alone had the power to control Reconstruction. Lincoln did not live long enough to fight out the issue. He was assassinated on April 14, 1865, months before the next session of Congress in December. His successor was left with the Lincoln blueprint.

That successor was Andrew Johnson of Tennessee. Lincoln had appointed him military governor of Tennessee; then, as a reward for his loyalty and to save the Republican party from the charge of "sectionalism," had made him vice president in 1864.

Johnson was thrust into the presidency at an extremely difficult time. He was faced with a South—an area four times the size of France—which now lay in ruins, devastated by gun and torch. Confederate soldiers, still straggling home during the summer of 1865, passed great farms that had been laid waste and abandoned; mansions and public buildings that were in ashes; streets, roads, and railroad lines that had been torn apart. Masters of plantations, former owners of many slaves, now labored in the fields themselves, trying desperately to grub enough food to keep their families alive. Blacks, expecting something tangible from their new freedom and getting almost nothing

Sketch shows a scene at the office of the Freedmen's Bureau in Richmond, Virginia, in 1866.

at all, took various courses. Some wandered from place to place, disillusioned, hungry, and ill. Others staked out small farms and began new lives. Still others, sensing their plight and deeply concerned, held conventions in various cities to discuss problems and map strategy.

On May 29 the president issued a proclamation of amnesty along the lines of Lincoln's but further excepting "all persons who have voluntarily participated in said rebellion and the estimated value of whose taxable property is over twenty thousand dollars."

Moving further, Johnson appointed provisional civilian governors in North and South Carolina, Georgia, Florida, Alabama, Mississippi, and Texas. (Arkansas, Louisiana, Tennessee, and Virginia already had "loyal" governments which Johnson recognized.) Then, in line with Lincoln's method, he ordered conventions held in those states. Ordinances of secession were to be repealed and new state constitutions were to be drawn in accordance with that of the United States, including a provision for the abolition of slavery. Blacks had no part in the move. State officials, all of them white, were elected and all-white legislatures were chosen. Before the end of the year, Johnson had completed "political reconstruction" of all the states of the old Confederacy (except Texas, which delayed action until the spring of 1866); and by December 18 all the legislatures, except Mississippi, had ratified the Thirteenth Amendment, which had been approved by Congress on January 31, 1865, and which abolished slavery throughout the Union.

When the December, 1865, session of Congress began, senators and representatives from nearly all the former Confederate states were in Washington ready to take their seats. Waiting to be seated was Alexander H. Stephens, who had been vice-president of the Confederacy. With him were four Confederate generals, five Confederate colonels, six Confederate cabinet officers and fifty-eight members of the Confederate Congress.

But in both the House and the Senate, the Radicals were on guard. Caucuses were held. Following a Radical plan, House Speaker Thaddeus Stevens instructed the clerk to omit from the roll call the name of every representative from a former Confederate state. The Senate, under the leadership of Charles Sumner, took the same course. Stevens and the other Radicals declared that Johnson was being too easy with the South. They said he had defied Congress by going ahead with Reconstruction during the congressional recess. In addition, he had given tacit approval to a series of "Black Codes" which had been enacted by the new state governments during the summer of 1865.

The codes set up a complex system of social, economic, and political controls. They dealt with labor contracts, apprenticeships, migration, vagrancy, civil and legal rights—every facet of black life. Black children separated from their parents could be made into quasi-slaves. Blacks could come into courts and testify as witnesses only in cases in which blacks were involved. Blacks could not possess firearms. Their employment was often limited to contract labor.

In Mississippi, which adopted particularly harsh codes, freedmen were required to have "lawful employment" and to sign contracts binding them to employers for an entire year. Any black found without this "lawful employment" was termed a "vagrant" and was subject to be seized and hired out by a sheriff to anyone who would pay his fine and be responsible for him.

The *Chicago Tribune* reacted to the Mississippi code by thundering on its editorial page: "We tell the white men of Mississippi that the men of the North will convert the State of Mississippi into a frog pond before they will allow such laws to disgrace one foot of soil in which the bones of our soldiers sleep and over which the flag of freedom waves."

This editorial echoed the sentiments of Stevens and Sumner and the other Radicals and Northerners sympathetic to blacks. The situation led to a February, 1866, meeting between the president and a delegation of black leaders. Journeying to the White House to ask Johnson's views on civil rights and black enfranchisement were several black spokesmen, including Frederick Douglass, George T. Downing

of Rhode Island, and John Jones of Illinois. Johnson made it clear that he opposed any federal law to protect freedmen. The black delegation was stunned. Douglass warned the president: "You enfranchise your enemies and disenfranchise your friends."

On March 14, 1866, both houses of Congress passed a Civil Rights Act which conferred citizenship on blacks ("all persons born in the U.S. and not subject to any foreign powers, excluding Indians not taxed.") It gave citizens "of every race and color" equal rights to make contracts, sue, testify in court, purchase, hold and dispose of property, and enjoy "full and equal benefit of all laws." Aimed at nullifying the Black Codes, the act made all citizens subject to "like punishment, pains, and penalties." Violation of the act was punishable by fine and/or imprisonment. Jurisdiction was given to U. S. District Courts, and power to arrest was given to U. S. marshals and attorneys. President Johnson, claiming that blacks were not yet ready for "the privileges and equalities of citizens," vetoed the act, but it was passed over his veto.

Then the Radicals pushed through Congress a resolution creating the Joint Committee on Reconstruction, a fifteen-member group which would study the situation in the South and come up with recommendations for new policy. The committee, composed of both Radical and Conservative Republicans, issued an eight-hundred-page report indicating that most Southern whites were still rebellious and had not sincerely accepted the results of the war. Blacks were being mistreated throughout the South, thus additional legislation—a Constitutional amendment—was needed to protect their rights.

The Fourteenth Amendment was proposed. This was a measure which: (1) incorporated the substance of the Civil Rights Act of 1866; (2) prohibited states from enacting laws which abridged the privileges or immunities of U.S. citizens, from depriving persons of life, liberty or property without due process, from denying any person the equal jurisdiction of U. S. laws; (3) enabled Congress to reduce a state's congressional representation when a state denied an adult male the right to vote for any reason other than crime or rebellion; (4) declared anyone who held federal or state office and had joined the Confederacy ineligible for public office until pardoned by two-thirds of Congress.

Schools for freedmen were opened in New Orleans (left), and other cities. Above: the first buildings of Howard University.

Black children studying their lessons on a Southern street in 1867.

While the amendment would not be ratified until 1868, it was passed by the House on May 10, 1866, and by the Senate on June 8, 1866. President Johnson denounced the amendment and urged Southern states not to ratify it. Tennessee ignored the advice and was readmitted to the Union.

Congress moved further in behalf of blacks by introducing a bill to strengthen and extend the life of the Freedmen's Bureau, the agency created on March 3, 1865, to assist newly freed slaves and war refugees. President Johnson vetoed the bill, claiming that Congress should not legislate for the states that were unrepresented in Congress. Instead of overriding the veto, Congress rewrote the bill and passed it in the face of another presidential veto.

Overriding of his vetoes and continued pressure from Congress so angered Johnson that he began a campaign of denunciation of the Radicals and all others opposed to his programs. He went on speaking tours, demanding that the nation send to Congress men who would support him. His attitude and his speeches seemed to encourage reactionary Southern whites to begin campaigns of terror against freedmen. During the summer of 1866, antiblack riots in Memphis and New Orleans left hundreds of blacks dead or seriously wounded and dozens of black schools, churches, and homes burned to the ground.

The disturbances, coupled with the president's appeals, seemed proof enough to Northerners that the South had learned nothing from the war and that blacks needed the protection that the ballot would bring. Northerners went to the

An 1866 drawing depicts life in the Colored Orphan Asylum in Memphis, Tennessee.

A white missionary teacher supervises a primary school for freedmen at Vicksburg, Mississippi.

polls on election day 1866 and delivered enough votes to give Republicans more than two-thirds majorities in both houses of Congress, thus checkmating reactionary forces and paralyzing Johnson's power to veto. On January 8, 1867, Congress passed a bill giving the vote to blacks in the District of Columbia. Three weeks later it passed a measure forbidding territorial legislatures from denying the ballot to blacks. Then it moved on the recalcitrant South with the Reconstruction Act of March 2, 1867, a measure designed to establish fair-minded, loyal governments in the former Confederate states. The act, and two supplementary acts, declared the existing Southern governments illegal and stipulated that all of the South except Tennessee, which had already won readmission to the Union, would be divided into five military districts. Each district would be under the command of a major general whose duty would be to prepare his district for readmission. Extremely important to the future of blacks was a provision that gave the commanders authority to "enroll qualified voters," while barring anyone disqualified by the Fourteenth Amendment. Protected by this provision, blacks flocked to voter registration places by the tens of thousands, thus placing themselves among the electorate that would choose delegates to conventions where new state constitutions would be drawn in line with U. S. laws.

In South Carolina, where blacks had the greatest political strength, they numbered 78,982 on voter registration lists as compared to 46,346 whites. Blacks were in the majority in twenty-one of the state's counties; whites were in the majority in ten. In Mississippi, registered voters numbered 60,167 blacks and 46,636 whites, with blacks in the majority in thirty-three of the state's sixty-one counties.

Congress completed its program of black suffrage in 1869 by passing the Fifteenth Amendment, which unequivocally declared: "The right of the citizens of the United States to vote shall not be denied or abridged by the United States or by any State on account of race, color, or previous condition of servitude." By 1870 the amendment had been debated in all the state legislatures and ratified.

Despite efforts by President Johnson to frustrate almost every one of its plans (efforts which provoked three separate attempts to impeach Johnson, the last defeated by merely one vote), Congress, by 1870, had supervised the registration of blacks and their participation at every level of state politics; had seen the framing of new state constitutions which incorated black thinking and provided for the protection of freedmen's rights; had watched as blacks were elected to the new state legislatures, and had welcomed black senators and representatives into congress.

By 1870, former slaves seemed indeed on their way to becoming free men.

One of the most significant acts by Congress in the closing months of the Civil War was the creation, in March, 1865, of the Bureau of Refugees, Freedmen, and Abandoned Lands. An arm of the War Department, the agency was directed by General Oliver Otis Howard and became known simply as the Freedmen's Bureau.

During the five years of its existence, during which its powers were increased by Congress, the bureau served as a sort of ombudsman for the nearly four million blacks freed from slavery and for countless whites who were war refugees. Food, clothing, and shelter were provided (more than 21 million rations were issued between 1865 and 1869). Within two years of the bureau's creation, it had set up forty-six fully staffed hospitals. (The death rate among freedmen was reduced from 38 percent in 1865 to 2.03 percent in 1869.) Freedmen were almost always denied fair treatment in the courts, so the bureau organized special courts and arbitration boards which had civil and criminal jurisdiction over minor cases involving freedmen. In addition, the bureau took over management of Southern lands that had been abandoned and/or confis-

Blacks gather for a celebration in Washington, D.C.

cated during the war. This land was leased, rented, or parceled out to freedmen, although much of it was returned to former white owners under the amnesty proclamations of Presidents Lincoln and Johnson. Actually, the bureau distributed barely a million acres of land in the South, while the government was giving out hundreds of millions of acres to homesteaders in the West.

Unquestionably, the greatest achievements of the Freedmen's Bureau were in education. Day schools, night schools, industrial schools, colleges, even Sunday schools—all were either set up or supervised by bureau personnel. And cooperation was given to various Northern religious and philanthropic organizations which established educational institutions in the South. Among the schools founded during the period were Howard University, Hampton Institute, Fisk University, Atlanta University, Tougaloo College, Storer College, St. Augustine's College, Tuskegee Institute, and Biddle Memorial Institute (renamed Johnson C. Smith University). By 1870, when the bureau halted its educational work, more than four thousand schools were educating black students, and more than five million dollars (a wholly inadequate sum, historians note) had been spent on the education of freedmen.

Critics of the bureau accused it not only of "interfering" with local authorities but of "corruption and inefficiency." But any fair assessment of the bureau's work will show that, despite shortcomings, despite inadequate funds from Congress, it was, for its time, an extraordinary aid to thousands of blacks struggling with the beginning of a new and uncertain life.

In addition to the Freedmen's Bureau, another agency offered relief and hope to blacks during the Reconstruction years. That agency was the black church, the first social institution controlled entirely by the nation's blacks, and one which gave them their first opportunity to develop leadership qualities.

The numerous Southern laws which had silenced black preachers and limited the growth of their congregations were removed by the victory of the North. These preachers were now free to evangelize. Their messages were full of promise and attracted thousands of those blacks who had worshiped with whites while sitting in segregated "crow's nests." Consequently, the black church grew rapidly and the influence of black preachers mushroomed. Older denominations such as the African Methodist Episcopal Church grew from twenty thousand members in 1856 to seventy-five thousand just one year after the war. Ten years later its membership had risen to two hundred thousand.

On the morning of May 2, 1866, whites invaded the black quarter of Memphis and shot many people.

The Baptists also experienced phenomenal growth. Numerous men felt the "call" and were ordained, and small Baptist churches sprang up throughout the South. Black Baptists of North Carolina were able to hold their first convention as early as 1866. Within a few years, such conventions were scheduled in every Southern state, and by 1870 Baptist church membership stood at more than five hundred thousand.

All the while, new church organizations were springing up. Black members of the white Primitive Baptist Church withdrew in 1865 to form the Colored Primitive Baptist Church of America. Four years later, the General Assembly of the Cumberland Presbyterian Church organized black members as the Colored Cumberland Presbyterian Church. Also to emerge was the Colored Methodist Episcopal Church, which by 1870 had grown large enough to organize five conferences and schedule a general conference for consecration of its first two bishops, R. H. Vanderhorst and W. H. Miles.

Out of these black church organizations came such early political leaders as Bishop J. W. Hood of North Carolina, Bishop H. M. Turner of Georgia, Bishop R. H. Cain of South Carolina, and the first black U.S. senators, Rev. Hiram R. Revels and Blanche K. Bruce. And of incalculable value was the spiritual refuge which these houses of worship provided to blacks in the post-Reconstruction period.

Four major civil rights acts were passed by Congress between 1866 and 1875.

The first Civil Rights Act was designed to protect blacks from racist state laws such as the Black Codes.

The 1870 Enforcement Act was a measure which imposed criminal sanctions for interference with the right of blacks to vote—a right granted under the Fifteenth Amendment. One section of the measure specified penalties for those who "go in disguise upon the public highway" to violate the civil rights of another. This

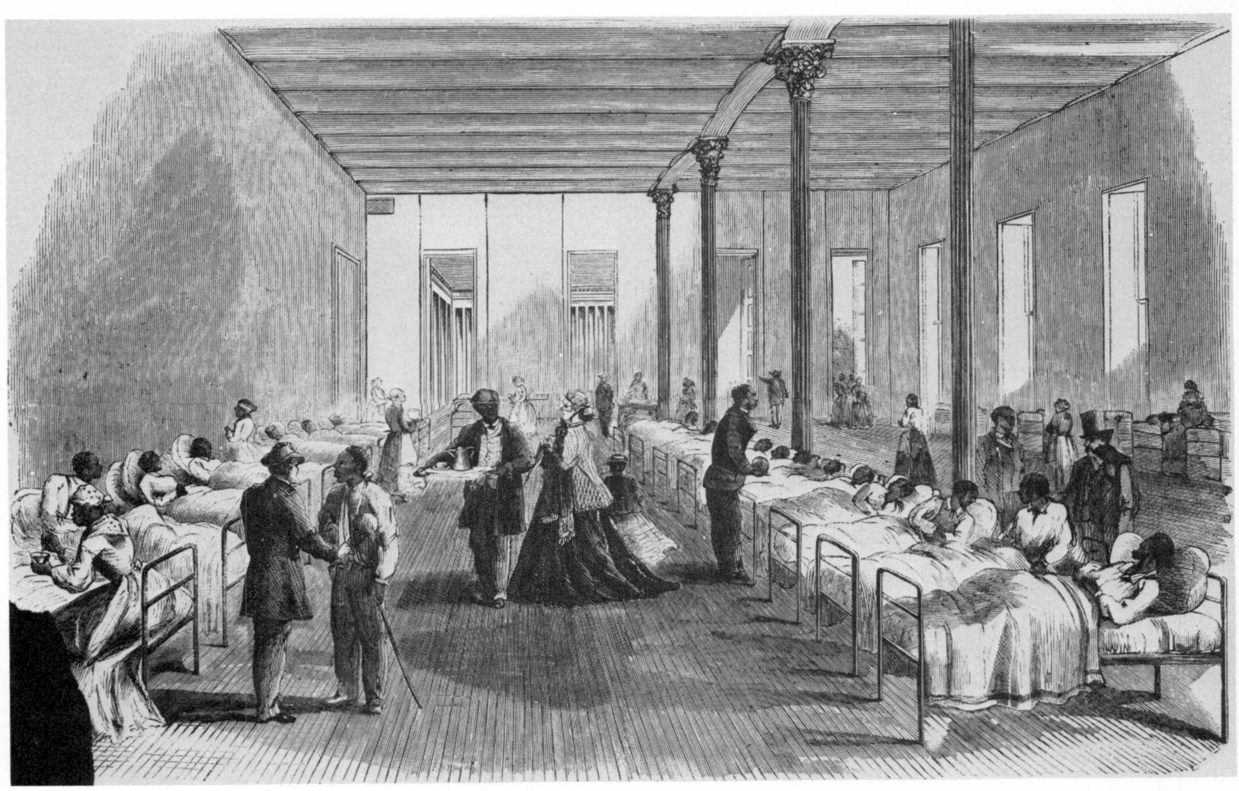

Riot victims were cared for in the New Orleans Marine Hospital while a Military Commission investigating the riot examined witnesses.

was a blow to members of the Ku Klux Klan and other racist groups.

Perhaps the most far-reaching of all the acts was the "Ku Klux Act," which set penalties for those who deprived "any person or any class of persons of the equal protection of the laws, or of equal privileges or immunities under the laws."

The last of these acts was the one of March 1, 1875, which included the provision that "all persons within the jurisdiction of the United States shall be entitled to the full and equal enjoyment of the accommodations, advantages, facilities, and privileges of inns, public conveyances on land or water, theaters, and other places of public amusement."

Significant parts of each of the latter three acts were declared unconstitutional by a Supreme Court which, by the late 1870s, reflected the nation's feeling, both South and North, that blacks had been given just about all the rights they ought to have. For example, the entire "public accommodations" section of the 1875 act was struck down in a landmark 1883 decision, virtually nullifying much of the Reconstruction era legislation.

Only one member of the Court dissented. That member was Justice John Marshall Harlan, and the words he wrote would, in years to come, be repeated many times:

Blacks and whites join in jubilation (above) after Civil Rights Bill is passed over the President's veto on April 9, 1866. The Capitol was the center of an intense struggle over Reconstruction policy.

> The [majority] opinion proceeds . . . upon grounds entirely too narrow and artificial . . . . Constitutional provisions, adopted in the interest of liberty . . . have been so construed as to defeat the ends the people desired to accomplish, which they attempted to accomplish, and which they supposed they had accomplished by changes in their fundamental law . . . . [The] court has departed from the familiar rule requiring, in the interpretation of constitutional provisions, that full effect be given to the intent with which they were adopted.

Congressional drafting of all the Reconstruction era civil rights acts was due mainly to two men—Senator Charles Sumner of Massachusetts and Representative Thaddeus Stevens of Pennsylvania.

It was Stevens, an unyielding opponent of presidential leniency toward Southern rebels, who had wrested control of Reconstruction from President Andrew Johnson and turned it over to Congress's Joint Committee on Reconstruction, which he dominated. Stevens exercised such strong control over Congress that he was considered for a time as the most powerful man in the nation's political life. Tall, stooped, afflicted with a club foot, Stevens was not, it is said, an attractive man. But his dedication was such that, in his final years, he insisted on being carried daily to his seat in the House to continue his fight until his death.

In the Senate, Sumner had fought for the civil rights acts with the same idealism and zeal with which he had fought in earlier days for the emancipation of slaves. He believed that blacks ought to have free public schools, free homesteads, and the vote, and insisted that Congress impose whatever measures necessary to force the South to acknowledge absolute equality of blacks. Together, Stevens and Sumner prodded Congress, criticized presidents, and demanded equal rights for blacks.

The fruit of Stevens' and Sumner's and other Radicals' labor provided the vital legal structure—and some semblance of a protective umbrella of federal concern—for blacks' dramatic progression from slavery to a freedom which gave them the power to demand respect as citizens.

BLACK RECONSTRUCTION WAS A time when blacks shared power in every former Confederate state, when they had absolute control of certain high offices, and when the sheer weight of their numbers at the polls forced white men to consider them and legislate many times in their favor. But the era was not, as some historians have claimed, one of "black rule."

For example, the total membership of nine of the constitutional conventions was 713 whites and a mere 260 blacks. In no state convention, except that of South Carolina, did blacks constitute the majority of delegates. In Louisiana, they were exactly one-half the ninety-eight members, but in Texas only nine blacks sat among the ninety framers of the new constitution. In most states, actual power was held by an alliance of blacks and whites, including Scalawags, the native-born Southern whites who claimed loyalty to the Union and who thus had been allowed to vote and hold office, and Carpetbaggers, the Northern whites. Conservative whites charged that Carpetbaggers had emigrated to the South, carrying few possessions except those stuffed into traveling bags made of carpet cloth (hence "Carpetbaggers"). This charge has been discredited by modern research. Some black members of the conventions were former slaves. Others had always been free. Still others had, like the white Carpetbaggers, moved from the North after the war. Many of the delegates, both black and white, were uneducated men, but they earnestly sought solutions to their states' problems. Many black delegates had about as much native talent as their white counterparts, and a number of blacks were men of superior intellect.

Black delegates strongly influenced the constitutional conventions, and the documents that were framed were the most progressive the South had ever known. All of the new constitutions abolished slavery, and most abolished property qualifications for voting and holding public office. A major issue at each convention was that of free public schools. This was an entirely new concept in the South, where education had generally been offered only to the upper class, and where taxation for any kind of public welfare was virtually unknown. Nevertheless, it was at these postwar conventions that the groundwork for a new educational system was laid. Further, each new constitution gave the vote to male residents of a state, except certain "hardcore" former Confederates.

Despite such moderation, some whites were violently opposed to black suffrage and black participation in the affairs of government. Terrorist groups such as the Ku Klux Klan organized a campaign of intimidation.

Although the vote had been given to them grudgingly and many exercised their rights at the risk of life and limb, Southern blacks continued flocking to the polls and black men by the dozens were elected to both state and national offices.

An example of black participation in governments of the former Confederate states is Mississippi, which established, between 1868 and 1874, the framework of a state government which was reform-oriented and in many ways democratic. Its constitutional convention of 1868 consisted of sixteen blacks and eighty-four whites. Working together, the black and white delegates framed a document which prohibited racial distinctions and put an end to property qualifications for voting and for jury duty.

Mississippi had been hit hard by the ravages of war and its credit was extremely bad. But within four years, a new legislature, 40 blacks out of 140 members

of both houses, established a good credit record and passed strong tax measures. The state university was reorganized, a biracial educational system was created and financed, and two black normal schools and a black university were founded. Old state office buildings were rehabilitated and construction began on new facilities for the physically handicapped and the insane. Every law based on race was repealed. Public accommodations were opened to all, regardless of race.

All this happened in the 1870s, during Black Reconstruction, in a state which

Thaddeus Stevens (above) and Charles Sumner were among the most persistent congressional leaders demanding rights for blacks during the Reconstruction era. Stevens was the architect of the Radical Reconstruction program.

had seen some of slavery's worst excesses. Faced with a tough Congress, however, Mississippi reversed its position and blacks began to rise. Black participation in the state's legislature foreshadowed a time when a black man, John R. Lynch, would serve as speaker of the Mississippi house. In 1873 blacks were elected to three important posts: A. K. Davis, lieutenant governor; T. W. Cardozo, superintendent of education, and James Hill, secretary of state.

The state sent to the U.S. Senate the only two blacks ever to serve in that body until Edward W. Brooke (R., Mass.), was elected in 1966. They were Hiram R. Revels and Blanche K. Bruce.

Revels was a Fayetteville, North Carolina, free black who was a minister in the African Methodist Episcopal Church. He migrated to Indiana, where he studied at a Quaker seminary, then to Drake County, Ohio, for additional seminary work, and finally to Illinois, where he graduated from Knox College in Bloomington. After preaching in the Midwest and in the Border States, he recruited blacks in Maryland for the Union Army. In 1863 he moved to St. Louis to open a large school for freedmen, then returned to Mississippi in 1864 as a Union Army chaplain. He settled in Natchez after the war as presid-

Portrait of Mrs. Lydia Smith, the black housekeeper of Representative Thaddeus Stevens. It is said that she not only ran his homes in Lancaster, Pennsylvania, and Washington, D.C., but influenced his actions in behalf of newly freed blacks.

ing elder of the African Methodist Episcopal Church and there began his political ascent, beginning with election to the Natchez City Council in 1868.

He was elected to the state senate and on January 20, 1870, the Mississippi legislature, under pressure from blacks, elected him to fill the unexpired U.S. Senate term of Confederate President Jefferson Davis. Revels, then forty-two, became a celebrity overnight.

After three days of Senate debate over his qualifications, Revels was admitted by a vote of forty-eight to eight, and people in the galleries rose as the nation's first black congressman walked down the aisle to be sworn in. The time was 4:40 P.M. on Friday, February 25, 1870. Three weeks later, Senator Revels delivered his maiden speech—one in which he opposed the readmission of Georgia to the Union without proper safeguards for its black minority. Later, however, Revels emerged as a "moderate" black who urged racial conciliation and favored removal of all the restrictions that Radical congressmen had placed on former Confederates.

Bruce, the state's other black senator, was a different sort of man—one, for example, who refused to use the word "colored," saying always "I am a Negro and proud of my race." He had been born a slave in Prince Edward County, Virginia, on March 1, 1841, and in 1861 escaped to Hannibal, Missouri, where he organized one of the first black schools. He left for Mississippi in 1869, knowing no one and with seventy-five cents in his pocket. But he had attended Oberlin College, spoke well, and was a man of impressive appearance. He caught the eye of Mississippi Governor James L. Alcorn, who made him sergeant-at-arms of the senate and then sent him to Bolivar County as assessor. There Bruce won election as sheriff and acquired a one-thousand-acre plantation. He served for a while as superintendent of public schools, then in the 1874 election was elected as U.S. Senator for a full term. He served from 1875–81 and introduced numerous bills to improve the condition of blacks; he also spoke against a bill restricting Chinese immigration and denounced the nation's treatment of American Indians. Bruce became one of the most respected members of the U.S. Senate and, in 1880, was proposed as a nominee for the vice-presidency. He withdrew in favor of Chester A. Arthur, who later became president. Bruce turned down appointments as minister to Brazil and third assistant postmaster general, but at the end of his term in 1881 accepted appointment from President James A. Garfield as registrar of the United States Treasury.

In an effort to force impeachment of President Andrew Johnson, Representative Stevens debates issue in the House of Representatives.

Here are some examples of black political participation in other Southern states:

South Carolina—In the first legislature after the war there were eighty-seven black men and forty white men. Two speakers of the house were black, Samuel J. Lee in 1872 and Robert B. Elliott in 1874, and three times a black man was chosen to act as president of the white-controlled senate. Two blacks served as lieutenant-governors, Alonzo J. Ransier in 1870 and Richard H. Gleaves in 1872. Secretary of state from 1868 to 1872 was Francis L. Cardozo, a brilliant, highly educated man who had studied at the University of Glasgow and in London. He also served as state treasurer from 1872 to 1876. Associate Justice J. J. Wright was the only black member of a state supreme court during Reconstruction. At one time, the South Carolina delegation in Congress was all-black. Joseph H. Rainey served five terms; Richard H. Cain, two; Robert Smalls, five; Thomas E. Miller, one; Robert C. DeLarge and Alonzo J. Ransier, one; Robert B. Elliott and George W. Murray, two.

Alabama—Blacks played minor roles in Alabama politics during Reconstruction. Even though twenty-six blacks sat in the house and one sat in the senate none gained a position of power. The state sent three blacks to Congress: Jere Haralson, Benjamin S. Turner, and James T. Rapier.

Louisiana—Between 1868 and 1896, 133 blacks sat in the Louisiana legislature. Thirty-eight were senators and ninety-five were representatives. Three blacks served as lieutenant-governors: Oscar J. Dunn, P. B. S. Pinchback and C. C. Antoine. The state elected John W. Menard as the nation's first black congressman, but on his arrival in the House on December 21, 1868, he was refused his seat. The reason, according to Congressman James A. Garfield of the Committee on Elections, was that it was "too early to admit a Negro to the U.S. Congress." The state later sent Charles E. Nash to the House where he served for two terms. Other high-ranking blacks included Secretary of State P. G. Deslonde, State Treasurer Antoine Dubuclet and Superintendent of Public Education W. G. Brown.

Georgia—Twenty-nine black representatives and three black senators elected to the Georgia legislature had to go to the state supreme court to establish their right to serve. They did not regain their seats until a full year after white members of the legislature in September, 1868, declared them "ineligible." Despite hostility from white members, they introduced progressive measures dealing with education, the jury system, reform of city government, and woman suffrage. Two blacks, Jefferson Long and H. M. Turner, led a losing battle for better wages for black workers. Long represented a Georgia district in Congress for a part of a term, and in 1869 Turner was named postmaster of Macon by President Grant.

FLORIDA—Blacks in the Florida legislature supported measures dealing with relief, education, and the right to vote. An outspoken champion of public schools was H. S. Harmon, and Jonathan Gibbs, secretary of state from 1868 to 1872, state superintendent of public instruction from 1872 to 1874. Josiah T. Walls served in Congress for two terms.

NORTH CAROLINA—While blacks attained no significant political positions during Reconstruction, black legislators—21 of 149 members—were influential in inauguration of the state's system of public schools. One legislator, the Rev. J. W. Hood, who had helped write the state constitution in 1868, was a leader in the field of education. The state sent John A. Hyman to Congress for one term and James E. O'Hara, H. P. Cheatham, and George H. White for two terms each.

VIRGINIA—Twenty-seven blacks sat in Virginia's first legislature after Reconstruction, but none achieved high positions in state government. Only one black, John M. Langston, served in the U.S. House for one term.

Tennessee, Arkansas, and Texas blacks had little influence on new governments and sent no blacks to Congress. In Arkansas, J. T. White was commissioner of public works and internal improvements, and J. C. Corbin was superintendent of schools.

The following table shows the participation of blacks in Congress from the beginning of Reconstruction to 1901:

CONGRESS	DATE	MEMBER	STATE
41st	1869–71	J. H. Rainey	S.C.
		J. F. Long	Ga.
		H. R. Revels	Miss.
42nd	1871–73	J. T. Walls	Fla.
		B. S. Turner	Ala.
		J. H. Rainey	S.C.
		R. C. DeLarge	S.C.
		R. B. Elliott	S.C.
43rd	1873–75	R. H. Cain	S.C.
		R. B. Elliott	S.C.
		A. J. Ransier	S.C.
		J. H. Rainey	S.C.
		J. T. Rapier	Ala.
		J. T. Walls	Fla.
		J. R. Lynch	Miss.
44th	1875–77	J. R. Lynch	Miss.
		B. K. Bruce	Miss.
		J. T. Walls	Fla.
		J. Haralson	Ala.
		J. A. Hyman	N.C.
		C. E. Nash	La.
		J. H. Rainey	S.C.
		Robert Smalls	S.C.
45th	1877–79	R. H. Cain	S.C.
		J. H. Rainey	S.C.
		Robert Smalls	S.C.
		B. K. Bruce	Miss.
46th	1879–81	B. K. Bruce	Miss.
47th	1881–83	Robert Smalls	S.C.
		J. R. Lynch	Miss.
48th	1883–85	J. E. O'Hara	N.C.
		Robert Smalls	N.C.
49th	1885–87	Robert Smalls	S.C.
		J. E. O'Hara	N.C.
51st	1889–91	T. E. Miller	S.C.
		J. M. Langston	Va.
		H. P. Cheatham	N.C.
52nd	1891–93	H. P. Cheatham	N.C.
53rd	1893–95	G. W. Murray	S.C.
54th	1895–97	G. W. Murray	S.C.
55th	1897–99	G. H. White	N.C.
56th	1899–1901	G. H. White	N.C.

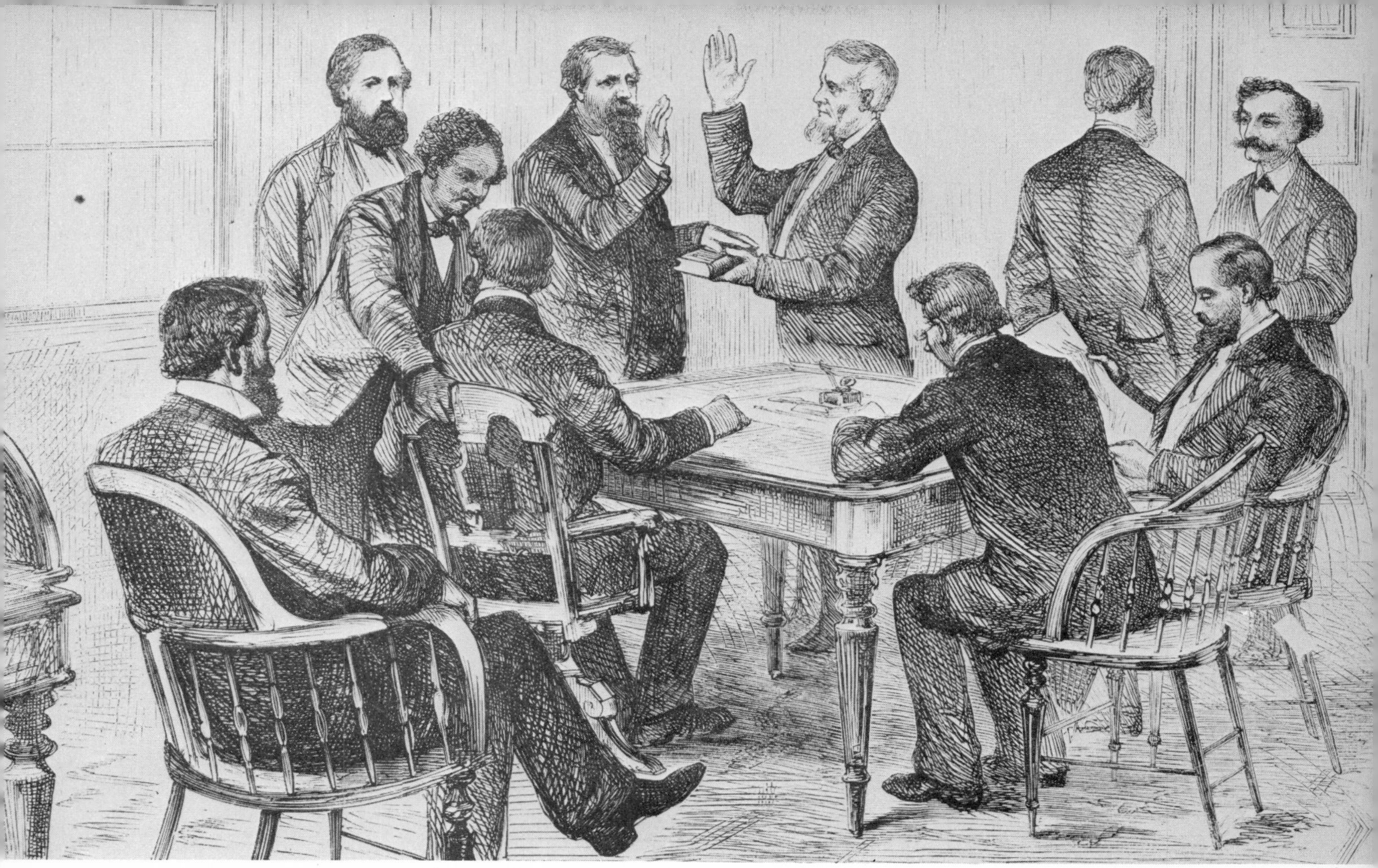

Gardane Cazanave takes the oath of office along with other members of the Louisiana Returning Board (above). Outside a North Carolina registration office in an early election.

A black politician delivers an election speech during the first days of balloting by blacks in the South.

While a certain school of historians has traditionally characterized black legislators of the Reconstruction Era as "ignorant and corrupt," no amount of anti-black propaganda can erase the constructive work of the Republican-black regimes. The new state constitutions adopted during Reconstruction were the most progressive codes by which the South had ever lived. As for the "ignorance" of the black men who helped write those codes, Lerone Bennett Jr. writes: "Although a degree may be necessary for writing about politics or teaching it, a degree is not at all necessary for practicing the game. A politician needs drive, energy, the ability to deal with people, the skills of the conference table and the smoky room, nerve, cheek and an eloquent tongue. Many black leaders [during Reconstruction] had these requisites."

And they had more. Carter G. Woodson and Charles H. Wesley reported in *The Negro In Our History*, "Some of the Negro officeholders had undergone considerable training and had experienced sufficient mental development to be able to discharge their duties with honor. Jere Haralson learned enough to teach. R. H. Cain studied at Wilberforce. James T.

Rapier was well educated in a Catholic school in Canada. Benjamin Turner clandestinely received a fair education in Alabama. James E. O'Hara obtained a secondary education. According to Frederick Douglass, Robert Brown Elliott, educated at Eton College, England, had no peer in his race except Samuel R. Ward. "Most Negroes who sat in Congress during the eighties and nineties, moreover, had more formal education than Warren G. Harding, once president of the United States."

As for being "corrupt," modern scholarship has shown that, while some blacks left office considerably richer than when they first ventured into politics, most were considerably more honest than their white counterparts.

From the very first days of Reconstruction, most Southerners waged war against the Reconstruction regimes. As early as 1866, long before blacks began their rise in politics, bands of white men had waged campaigns of terror against freedmen and their white supporters who had come down from the North. Just one year after the end of the war, the head of the Freedmen's Bureau in Georgia had complained that whites calling themselves Jayhawkers, Regulators and the Black Horse Cav-

The registration of black voters in Richmond during the first municipal election after the Civil War.

alry combed the state, committing "the most fiendish and diabolical outrages." One after another, various "protective societies" had been formed by whites. Since the most notorious of these "societies" were the Ku Klux Klan and the Knights of the White Camellia, perhaps some attention should be given them.

The Klan was started in Pulaski, Tennessee, a year after the close of the Civil War. With former Confederate General Nathan Bedford Forrest as its leader, the Ku Klux Klan was formed as the "Invisible Empire of the South."

Throughout the South KKK "dens" were formed and terror campaigns began. Intimidation was the chief weapon, but for those blacks who refused to be frightened the Klan resorted to kidnappings, whippings, torture, and murder.

Like the Ku Klux Klan, the Knights of the White Camellia had as their principal aim the maintenance of white supremacy in the South despite Reconstruction laws. Founded in New Orleans in 1867, the Knights' organizational structure closely resembled that of the Klan, and the same tactics of terrorism and reprisal were employed to block the increasing political and economic power of blacks.

But with their new freedom, many blacks refused to recognize the old social codes, refused to knuckle under to the "white superiority" idea. While there are no reliable figures on the number of blacks who acquired land during Reconstruction, it is known that it was not unusual for them to own and manage plantations of a thousand acres or more. Some of the big landowners such as Blanche K. Bruce and James T. Rapier were politicians. Others were farmers who discovered ways to fight their way up and form the *avant garde* of a black entrepreneurial class which flourished for a few years. There are reports of successful independent black farmers throughout the South. One observer noted that, by the mid-seventies, blacks of Georgia owned "nearly 400,000 acres of farming real estate, besides city property."

Fearing the growing independence of these black farmers, white planters organized combines to protect their own interests. Some planters refused to sell land to blacks, and those who employed blacks conspired to fix wages and blacklist any worker who complained. Workers fought back with sit-down demonstrations and strikes and by refusing to renew labor contracts. Some angry black workers burned fields, barns, and planters' homes.

Blacks also organized various labor conventions which resolved that blacks should not work as laborers and that they should refuse to pay more than $1.50 an acre for farm land. One such convention in Alabama urged that sharecropping be ended and that a uniform system of written labor contracts be instituted. It was better, some believed, to work for a fixed wage than enter into the sharecropper sys-

John W. Menard, the first black man elected to the House of Representatives, received premature congratulations from congressmen on December 21, 1868. Elected from Louisiana, he was denied his seat in the House.

tem which was exploiting black families by the thousand. Many of the South's huge plantations had been broken up into smaller farms and offered for sale to whites. These white farmers would then permit destitute black families to move onto the property and work the land. But blacks had no money to buy seed, tools, and food. White financiers would loan money to the farm owner for purchase of these needs, which would in turn be offered to the black family in exchange for a "share" of whatever crops were raised. Always when accounts were settled after harvest, the usually illiterate "sharecropper" found his "account" overdrawn—he had been advanced more seed, tools, and food than his share of the crop was worth. All bookkeeping was, of course, done by the white farm owner, who would demand that the black family wipe out the debt by remaining and raising another crop the following year. By the time the next crop was harvested, the debt was bigger than before. Numerous black families tried to escape the system but were jailed and fined. Fines were paid by going back to the same farm and working, usually at less than a dollar a day. One resolution after another passed at the labor conventions warned against this return to the old master-slave relationship. But because whites had arranged to offer only the worst land to blacks and because the majority of blacks were economically trapped, sharecropping was the only answer for most. A series of bad crops, the depression of 1873, and a growing climate of hostility forced additional thousands into this sharecropper class by 1875.

A few black independent farmers managed to hold on, however, and grew rich.

Blacks (left) debate the issues in the South Carolina legislature of 1873. Below: a mixed jury in 1867.

Blanche K. Bruce was the first black to serve a full term (1875–81) in the U.S. Senate. P. B. S. Pinchback (below), served briefly as governor of Louisiana.

Hiram Rhodes Revels of Mississippi was the first black United States Senator (1870–71).

One example is Benjamin T. Montgomery, who bought the Jefferson Davis plantation at Davis Bend, Mississippi, and lived in splendor in the baronial mansion of the former president of the Confederacy.

Similar black enterprise was noted in other areas during the first ten years of Reconstruction despite intimidation. Black laborers virtually monopolized work in the building trades and along the wharves. They flocked to the tobacco factories of Virginia and to South Carolina's industrial plants. Most teamsters were black men, and so were many of the South's skilled masons, carpenters, cabinetmakers, etc. One estimate is that at least 100,000 of the region's 120,000 skilled workers were black.

With money earned from their labor, many blacks began opening their own business enterprises—barber shops, restaurants, general stores, etc.—which served all races alike. South Carolina Congressman Richard J. Cain became one of the biggest real estate brokers in Charleston, and Mississippi's secretary of state, James Hill, engaged in various land and real estate deals.

One attempt to thwart white efforts to limit black independence was the formation of a number of independent corporations and cooperatives. In Virginia, the Mount Alto Mining and Land Company was organized. In South Carolina and Louisiana, blacks got together in cooperatives and bought and ran huge plantations. In a number of cities similar cooperatives bought up land and houses which were then sold to members at relatively low prices. One of the most outstanding examples of cooperative enterprise was the Chesapeake Marine and Dry Dock Company which was organized by black caulkers, mechanics, and carpenters who had been refused work on the Baltimore docks. Together, the blacks bought a shipyard and marine company which was soon doing more repair work than any firm of its kind in the city.

The cooperative movement, the burgeoning black business enterprises, black support of black political candidates, the formation of black labor unions, the growth of black religious organizations and associations of all kinds—all were expressions of the sense of blackness and "peoplehood" which rapidly developed during the Reconstruction Era.

Economic and political activity was only the beginning. Education became a priority. Not only children but grown men and women packed the schools. Re-

J. H. Rainey (S.C.)

Robert B. Elliott (S.C.)

J. T. Walls (Fla.)

A composite drawing of seven blacks who served in the U.S. Congress during Reconstruction.

J. T. Rapier (Ala.)

R. H. Cain (S.C.)

J. R. Lynch (Miss.)

porters traveling through the South observed blacks "studying everywhere—on the wharves, in the fields, in the kitchen." Sometimes three generations—grandmother, mother, and child—were found in the same classroom.

While many of the schoolteachers were white Northerners employed by the Freedmen's Bureau, and while white Northern philanthropists provided funds for the establishment of many schools, blacks usually retained control.

Integrated schools were not a rarity. In the larger cities black and white children attended school together. After a visit to a school in New Orleans, George W. Cable, a white Southerner, wrote:

> I saw to my great and rapid edification, white ladies teaching Negro boys; colored women showing the graces and dignity of mental and moral refinement, youth of both races standing in the same classes and giving each other peaceable, friendly, effective competition; and black classes, with black teachers, pushing intelligently up into the intricacies of high-school mathematics.

Perhaps nothing angered Ku Klux Klansmen and other racists more than the school integration and the black-white social mixing that could be found throughout the South. Integration was found in bars, railroad cars, and in all kinds of amusement places. Blacks who could afford to do so bought fine homes in "white" neighborhoods. Black men married white women and white men who had long kept secret their romances with black women now brought these relationships into the open. More than one white woman was whipped by the Klan after being seen in the company of a black man. Some white men who insisted on marrying black women were actually killed.

How did whites react to all this? Some accepted it. Others were so disgusted that they packed up their belongings and headed West. Many supported the activities of the Klan and the other secret "societies." Every weapon was used—violence, intimidation, social ostracism, economic pressure, trickery, and lies—and every inch of black progress was made against a background of racist terror.

The favorite targets of masked night riders were black voters and their white supporters, black local officials, teachers, and the black independent farmers. One after another, blacks active in Republican politics were picked off—run out of town, compromised, or killed.

There is no record of how many black men died in sleepy Southern villages, but it is estimated that there were thousands.

Individual murder was not enough. Massacres occurred in a number of towns. Thirty black men were killed in the Meridian, Mississippi, massacre of 1871. Teachers of black students were dragged into woods and whipped, then their schools were burned. Black farmers' crops were seized or burned. Economic power was brought to bear. Black Republicans could not find work, stores refused to sell to their wives, doctors refused to treat their children. As for white Republicans, they were socially ostracized. Their wives were humiliated on the streets and at church. Soon whites by the thousands began switching to the Democratic party.

Black Republicans who wavered or who actually donned the distinctive red shirts of the Democrats in order to survive came under attack from black women. Landladies evicted them. Black women refused to marry them, talk to them, or sleep with them. One South Carolina wife spelled it out. She had no intention, she said, of sleeping with "a Democratic nigger." Women often spotted black Democrats on the streets, rushed up and shouted "Uncle Tom," then tore off the red shirt. Some blacks formed rifle clubs for protection. But many were stripped of their weapons by white sheriffs. Others were too poor to buy guns.

J. J. Wright

F. L. Cardoza

H. M. Turner

Mifflin Gibbs

J. C. Corbin

J. W. Hood

J. T. White

J. J. Spelman

While little could be done to counteract the smear campaigns and the legal actions, both state and federal governments could have invoked provisions of the various Reconstruction acts to minimize the violence. But governors hesitated, and their hesitation made white reactionaries even more bold. Most of the governors refused to arm their state militia or utilize National Guard forces. Despite repeated requests from their legislatures, the Republican governors of Alabama, Mississippi, and Florida refused to organize militias. Other governors took the action, then lost their nerve and refused to order crackdowns. A notable exception was Governor William G. Brownlow of Tennessee who mobilized his militia and announced that whites had created a situation which required "a large amount of hanging." Another governor, Powell Clayton of Arkansas, mobilized his militia and declared martial law in 1868.

On the national level, President Ulysses S. Grant (who had been elected in 1868 with overwhelming black support) finally took action in 1871. He suspended the writ of habeas corpus and ordered arrests. Thousands of white citizens—including ministers and college presidents—were taken into custody for Klan violence. Some 5,172 men were tried in 1871–72, and 1,432 were sent to prison.

The president's action somewhat blunted the thrust of the terror campaigns, but there was reaction in the North. Northern whites, many of whom had grown tired of "the eternal nigger problem," began sympathizing with Southerners, who claimed "persecution" by President Grant. The Southern public relations effort convinced Northern industrialists and financiers that the racial troubles stood in the way of maximum exploitation of Southern resources.

Such respected journals as the New York *Commercial and Financial Chronicle*, the New York *Tribune*, and the *Nation* demanded an end to Reconstruction because it was "paralyzing southern business and discouraging those with capital to invest in that section."

By 1874, Democratic gains in the North had given Democrats a majority in the House of Representatives—the first Republican political defeat in a national election since the Civil War. Instead of giving additional federal protection to blacks, the House now refused to pass an army appropriation bill in order to force President Grant to withdraw the remaining federal troops in the South.

In 1875, Governor Adelbert Ames begged Grant's attorney general, Edward Pierrepont, to protect black voters during that year's election. But the federal government refused to act after being visited by a delegation of Republicans from Ohio, where an election was also being held. White sentiment in Ohio was

James A. Healy (above) was consecrated Bishop of Portland, Maine, in 1875, the first black American to become a Roman Catholic bishop. Bishop Healy's brother, Rev. Patrick Francis Healy S.J., Ph.D. (r.), was the only black president of Georgetown University, Washington, D.C.

such, the president was told, that if he sent troops to Mississippi the Republican party would lose Ohio. The decision was to save Ohio and leave Mississippi blacks to fend for themselves. In his reply to Ames, Pierrepont remarked that the people were "tired of these annual autumnal outbreaks in the South."

The result in Mississippi was that, throughout the state, blacks were beaten, shot, and intimidated in every way. Most were unable to cast a ballot unless accompanied by a white man who vouched that the vote would be for a Democrat. The Democrats took the state by a landslide. Commented President Grant: "Mississippi is governed today by officials chosen through fraud and violence, such as would scarcely be accredited to savages, much less to a civilized and Christian people."

Outside the South, blacks were having trouble, too. Many had moved from the South to urban areas in the North. Among the migrants were blacksmiths, bricklayers, harbor pilots, cabinetmakers, painters and other skilled workers. Laborers by the thousand had migrated, too. In seeking work they now found themselves in competition with whites—many of them European immigrants who had flooded Northern industrial cities during the war—who felt their job security threatened by the black influx. The situation was exacerbated by Northern industrialists who employed black workers to undermine white labor unions. The attempts of blacks to join white unions were defeated. Not until after 1880 would black workers be admitted in substantial numbers by organized labor. Meanwhile they would be regarded by angry whites as strikebreakers.

One of the most significant postwar economic efforts was the creation, in 1865, by the federal government, of the Freedmen's Savings and Trust Company. The bank's business was to be confined to blacks and two-thirds of its deposits would be invested in U. S. securities. The bank opened its doors in New York on April 4, 1865. Shortly there were branches in Nashville, New Orleans, Vicksburg, Louis-

Adelbert Ames (l.), a Reconstruction governor of Mississippi, and Robert K. Scott, a Republican governor of South Carolina.

Aboard ship, a few blacks joined the early northward stream of black families. *The New Orleans Tribune* (below), the first black daily newspaper, was published in French and English editions.

LA TRIBUNE DE LA NOUVELLE-ORLEANS.

JOURNAL POLITIQUE, PROGRESSISTE ET COMMERCIAL.

New Orleans Tribune.

A TRI-WEEKLY PAPER.

NEW ORLEANS, THURSDAY, JULY 21st, 1864. VOL. 1—No. 1.

ville, and Memphis. By 1872 there were thirty-four branches—all of them in the South, except the New York and Philadelphia branches. Deposits in all branches totaled $3,299,201 by 1874, the year the bank closed its doors. The bank failed because of faulty bookkeeping and a rash of bad loans. A run on the bank followed the Panic of 1873 and most of the top officials resigned. The few blacks who had been hired (none were offered positions when the bank first opened) were left to take the blame. Not even Frederick Douglass, who was made president in March, 1874, could save the institution in which so many blacks had placed hope and dreams. On

The National Colored Convention met in Washington, D.C., in 1869.

June 28, 1874, the Freedmen's Bank closed its doors. Thousands of black depositors suffered losses.

By the time of the presidential election of 1876, both Radical Republicanism and Reconstruction had run their course. Black political organizations had been smashed in almost all states of the South and tens of thousands of blacks had either been "persuaded" to join the Democratic party or had been frightened away from the polls. In Washington, most of the old Radical leaders were either dead or had lost their Congressional seats.

After little more than ten years, the back of a great movement for social reform had been broken. One by one the former Confederate states had been returned to the hands of white Democrats. One by one they had been "redeemed," the South's euphemism for white supremacy. Tennessee had come under Democrat control in 1869; Virginia and North Carolina in 1870; Georgia in 1871; Alabama, Arkansas, and Texas in 1874, and Mississippi in 1875. Now in 1876, the centennial of American independence, the old coalition of blacks, "Carpetbaggers" and "Scalawags" maintained control in only South Carolina, Florida, and Louisiana.

Since Mississippi had been captured

through the suppression of the black majority by an armed white minority, whites decided to use the same tactic to "redeem" the last three strongholds of black power.

Actually, by 1876 white Democrats held commanding positions in the Louisiana house and the Florida senate. Only South Carolina with its huge black bloc was still solidly Republican. There were 415,000 blacks and only 289,000 whites in the state. In the legislature, there were twenty-seven black men. One-half of Governor Daniel H. Chamberlain's cabinet was black. A black man, Robert Brown Elliott, served as both the speaker of the house and chairman of the Republican state executive committee.

In the fall elections, Chamberlain headed a Republican ticket of four black men and four white men. The Democratic opponent was Wade Hampton. Similarly, in Florida, Governor M. L. Stearns was opposed by Democrat G. F. Drew; and in Louisiana, Republican Stephen B. Packard faced F. T. Nichols.

Nationally, the Republicans had nominated Ohio Governor Rutherford B. Hayes to run for president against the Democratic nominee Samuel J. Tilden, the governor of New York.

In the South, Democrats scurried from state to state, making plans, plotting the strategy of "white supremacy." South Carolina's General M. W. Gary drew up a master plan based on methods that had been used in Mississippi. Among Gary's recommendations:

> Every Democrat must feel honor bound to control the vote of at least one Negro, by intimidation, purchase, keeping him away or as each individual may determine, how he may best accomplish it.
>
> Never threaten a man individually. If he deserves to be threatened, the necessities of the time require that he should die. A dead Radical is very harmless—a threatened Radical or one driven off by threats from the scene of his operations is often very troublesome, sometimes dangerous, always vindictive.

The Gary plan was adopted not only in South Carolina but in Florida and Louisiana. Whites armed themselves. The key state, South Carolina, was an armed camp. All able-bodied white South Carolinians were enrolled in rifle clubs, and thousands of whites wearing the Democrat red shirt marched through the streets of major towns and rode through the countryside.

South Carolina was locked in terror during the months leading up to the election. Black officials were shot down in the streets. Black voters were lynched. At a

Ku Klux Klan members are pictured in their garb, December, 1868. A cartoon (below) depicts white terror.

massacre in the town of Hamburg on July 8, 1876, six black men were murdered by being shot and stabbed. One had his tongue cut out. At another massacre in Ellerton, thirty-nine blacks died.

The South Carolina terror was so widespread that President Grant issued a proclamation commanding white rifle clubs to disband. Instead, they adopted new names: First Baptist Church Sewing Circle, Allendale Mounted Baseball Club, Mother's Little Helpers, and the like. Grant rushed federal troops to the state, but the troops sided with whites who invited them into their homes, introduced them to their daughters and made them "one of the family."

On election day, November 7, 1876, terror and fraud were in the air. As in Mississippi, blacks were intimidated into staying away from polling places, while whites (some of them having crossed from neighboring states) voted two or three times.

Democrats claimed victory throughout the South, and whites poured into the streets, shouting and cheering. But in South Carolina and Louisiana, the election was hotly contested and both Democrats and Republicans claimed victory and established governments.

Nationally, Tilden won 184 electoral votes—one short of a majority. Hayes won only 169 electoral votes. The presidency hung on the disputed votes in the South.

The ultimate electoral authority in the disputed states was the state returning boards in which blacks and Republicans still played key roles. These boards were empowered to go behind the returns and throw out all ballots which were, in board members' opinions, illegally cast. The returning boards met in South Carolina, Louisiana, and Florida and certified the election of Republican slates and Hayes electors. White Southerners went into a rage, refusing to accept the results. Too many plans had been made, too much blood shed, for a Southern loss now. For several months there were two governors and two legislatures in South Carolina and Louisiana. It seemed likely that there might be two U.S. presidents, too. There was talk of insurrection, of an Army *coup d'état*. Fearing that the nation was about to disintegrate, Democrats and Republicans agreed to the formation of an Electoral Commission composed of five associate justices of the Supreme Court and five members of Congress. The commission decided in favor of Hayes. Furious, the South mounted a filibuster in Congress, threatening to prevent the orderly counting of the electoral votes in the House of Representatives. In that case, if the filibuster continued past inauguration day, the nation would be without a president. Another civil war might be the result.

The South's price for peace was, for blacks, high indeed. The demand was that the Hayes Administration must: (1) remove all remaining federal troops from the South; (2) include at least one Southerner in the Cabinet; (3) give conservative Southern Democrats control of part of local patronage, and (4) support generous appropriations for internal improvements, particularly railroads, in the South.

The bargain was signed and sealed after a series of meetings which began in December, 1876, and lasted until a final meeting on February 26, 1877, in a room of the Wormley House, a Washington, D.C., hotel owned by a wealthy black businessman. While the Southerners had been given President Hayes' solemn word, they insisted that something be delivered in writing. This was done. A letter read:

> GENTLEMEN: Referring to the conversation had with you yesterday in which Governor Hayes' policy as to the status of certain Southern states was discussed, we desire to say in reply that we can assure you in the strongest possible manner of our great desire to have adopted such a policy as will give to the people of the States of South Carolina and Louisiana the right to control their own affairs in their own way; and to say further that we feel authorized, from an acquaintance with and knowledge of Governor Hayes and his views on this question, to pledge ourselves to you that such will be his policy.

The White League, an organization of white terrorists, attacks policemen and militia in an abortive attempt to take over the Louisiana state government in 1874.

The South was satisfied. The filibuster was called off, and Rutherford Birchard Hayes was inaugurated.

Hayes moved quickly to keep his promises to the South and to show the region that he was its friend. He appointed former Confederate General David M. Key as postmaster general, then proceeded with the promised withdrawal of the few troops remaining in South Carolina and Louisiana. Troops were pulled out of South Carolina on April 10, thus toppling the Republican government of Daniel H. Chamberlain. Fourteen days later, on April 24, the same move was made in Louisiana, and the Republican government of S. B. Packard fell. Then began a months-long campaign of "reconciliation" with the South. Numerous Southerners, including many former Confederates, were appointed to federal jobs, and Hayes made several trips into the South.

President Rutherford B. Hayes was the architect of the Compromise of 1877. White men (left), led by L. A. Wiltz, took possession of the speaker's chair in the Louisiana house of representatives on January 4, 1875.

The South's new Democratic government moved quickly to throw out the progressive Reconstruction era state constitutions and draft new ones which drastically slashed state services, crippled the system of free public education, disenfranchised blacks, and devised tax systems that soaked the poor, both black and white.

Among the most effective of all of the New South's moves were those which stifled the black vote. Since complete disfranchisement by state legislation was difficult because of the Fourteenth and Fifteenth amendments, a variety of extralegal methods of intimidation were used. In many towns, blacks were not allowed to show their faces on election day. Some Southerners objected to continued dependence on terror tactics to maintain white supremacy and Democrat power, but lynchings and burnings continued.

One of the most blatant of all efforts to thwart the Fifteenth Amendment was the writing into election laws of a "Grandfather Clause." No person could vote unless he was a descendant of someone who had voted prior to 1866.

Only a few areas of the South remained for a time as Republican strongholds, and it was these areas that produced the handful of blacks who held local, state, and national offices until the first year of the new century.

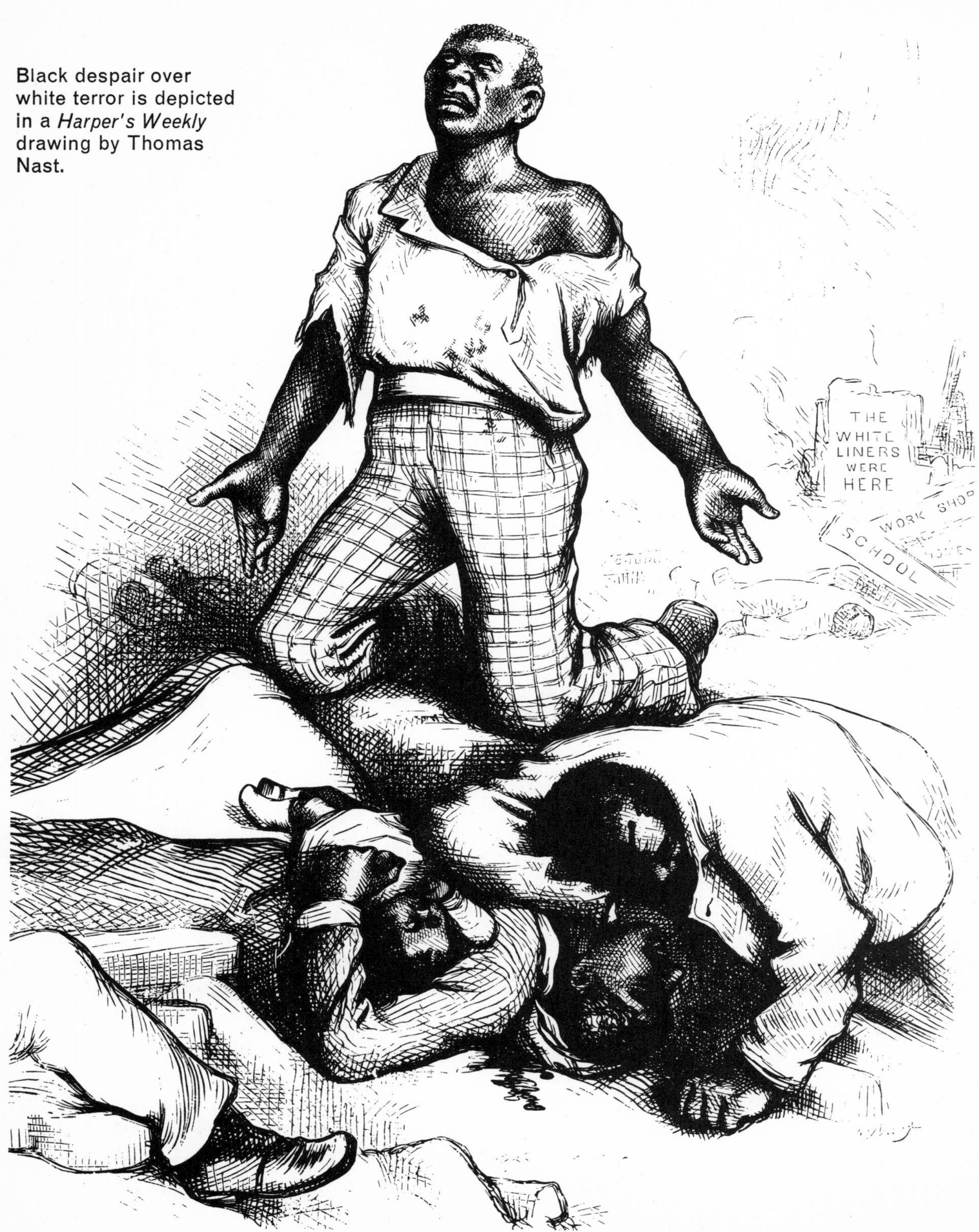

Black despair over white terror is depicted in a *Harper's Weekly* drawing by Thomas Nast.

2

Reaction and Renewal

THE POST-RECONSTRUCTION YEARS and the activities of blacks during the time have been somewhat neglected by historians. Thus many have the impression that disaffection with Republicanism, disappointment at the loss of political power and harsh treatment by white Democrats made blacks lapse into passivity after the inauguration of Rutherford B. Hayes. The fact is that this was one of the most active periods in black history. Blacks, both South and North, frequently and seriously challenged the nation's new political and economic priorities, and the Republican party was subject to particularly severe questioning. Numerous black organizations were formed and one proposal after another was made for redress of wrongs. Actions ranged from Chicago newspaper editor (*The Conservator*) Ferdinand Lee Barnett's 1878 demand that the word Negro no longer be spelled with a small *n*—"This breach of orthography is the white man's mark of disrespect," he said, ". . . [so] spell it with a capital!"—to the antilynching crusade of Barnett's wife, Ida B. Wells, who was forcibly driven out of Memphis because of her outspokenness. From black individuals, from black organizations and conventions, from black newspapers, etc. came various schemes for migration and emigration, plans for schools of all kinds, suggestions for the forming of labor unions, strategies for dealing with terror

in the South and quelling racial hostility in the North, and other measures for battling the white oppression that had descended like a blanket on the South.

For many blacks wishing to flee this oppression and the harshness of life as sharecroppers, migration seemed the only answer. Thus, in the late 1870s, began the first large upheaval of blacks in the nation's history. Thousands of black families merely moved from one part of the South to another; from plantations to cities; from worn-out lands to richer lands, and from "bad" states to "better" ones. This had been preceded by various small movements of blacks, especially adventurous cowboys, who had roamed the Texas

After 1900, blacks were lynched in both North and South. These photographs were taken in Duluth, Minnesota (top) and Marion, Indiana.

Early emigrants from the South to Liberia, these 325 left Savannah, Georgia, on March 1, 1896.

plains and the Indian Territory for a number of years. Some blacks had joined in the general westward expansion and had moved to the Southwest early in the decade. Even in the northern ranges a black man was no novelty during the mid-seventies. A few blacks had made their way to the Rockies and beyond to the California mining country, and some had even toyed with the idea of forming a separate state in order to escape discrimination. (The "separate state" idea was actually proposed in 1890 by the Texas Farmers' Colored Association, and the Oklahoma Territory was the choice. The all-black town of Langston, Oklahoma, was established in line with this idea in 1891, and all-black Boley, Oklahoma, was founded in 1904).

But the 1879 "exodus" was the largest movement, and two figures involved in it were Benjamin "Pap" Singleton, a Tennessee-born former slave who became an undertaker and head of the Tennessee Real Estate and Homestead Association, and Henry Adams, an influential black leader in Shreveport, Louisiana. Within a

Moses "Pap" Singleton was a leading figure in the migration movement to the Midwest.

The Missouri Mission Conference of the Methodist Church met in New Orleans in 1866.

few months, at least fifty thousand blacks left the South—almost all of them heading for Kansas. Kansas was chosen partly because of its association with the martyred abolitionist John Brown. Handbills describing opportunities in "Sunny Kansas" were distributed throughout the South by black railroad porters and steamboat hands, and Singleton, who was a persuasive speaker, roamed the South urging blacks to "get out." Henry Adams's colonization council reportedly recruited ninety-eight thousand blacks in Louisiana, Mississippi, Alabama, and Texas, all

The first buildings of Fisk University were former military barracks.

of whom said they wanted to leave the South even if "we have to run away and go into the woods."

Despite opposition from some leaders, throngs of blacks headed North. White Southerners began clamping down. Transportation companies refused to sell tickets to blacks. Vagrancy laws were used to arrest black travelers. Anyone caught preaching migration was horsewhipped and driven out of town. Southern whites accused Northern Republicans of enticing blacks away in order to strengthen Republican voter rolls in the North, and Congress appointed a committee to investigate the charge. Both Singleton and Adams joined others in giving testimony in Washington. What were the reasons for migration? While some 1,700 pages of testimony were taken, the essential reason was recorded in Senate Report 693 of the Forty-Sixth Congress:

> They stated that they had no security for life, limb or property; that they worked year in and year out and, notwithstanding they raised good crops, they were at the end of the year in debt; that they were charged exorbitant prices for provisions. . . . Men were shot down for political purposes. . . . They said they would rather go into the open prairie and starve.

By the end of 1879—following an extremely bad crop year, a devastating yellow fever epidemic, and more than the usual amount of violence from whites—thousands upon thousands of blacks had arrived in Kansas. Meeting hostility there, some had moved on to Missouri, Iowa, and Nebraska.

Still, the blacks came in droves. Some acquired land under the Homestead Act, but most spent long periods in poverty, aided only by the Freedmen's Relief Association and a few donations from Northern friends. Neither the state of Kansas nor the federal government offered meaning-

Virginia Hall, Hampton Institute, around 1874.

The first buildings of Atlanta University (above) and Tougaloo College's Berkshire Cottage, 1899.

ful assistance. But despite the poverty, despite the hostility, despite the harshness of winters in an unfamiliar land, few blacks returned to the South. The "exodus" continued until word filtered back to the South that Kansas weather was so harsh that many blacks were dying from exposure, that whites were racist even outside the South, and that jobs were extremely few.

At about the same time, an emigration plan was forming in the mind of the African Methodist Episcopal Church's Bishop Henry McNeal Turner, a former Union chaplain who could not forgive the nation for what he considered "ungrateful" treatment of blacks. Bishop Turner hated the racism of Southern whites and encouraged blacks to leave the United States and go to a foreign land and develop a nation of their own. Said Bishop Turner:

> *There is no manhood future in the United States for the Negro.* He may eke out an existence for generations to come, but he can never be a *man*—full, symmetrical and undwarfed. Upon this point I know thousands who make pretensions to scholarship, white and colored, will differ and may charge me with folly, while I in turn pity their ignorance of history and political and civil sociology. . . . The colored man who will stand up and in one breath say that the Negroid race does not want social equality and in the next predict a

Tuskegee Institute's principal, Booker T. Washington (center), poses with his faculty in 1897.

These photographs show the site (above) of Tuskegee Institute, and (below) Foster Hall and DeForest Chapel of Talladega College in 1909.

John Merrick, C. C. Spaulding, and Dr. A. M. Moore were the early management team of the North Carolina Mutual and Provident Association, now the North Carolina Mutual Life Insurance Company.

great future in the face of all the proscription of which the colored man is the victim, is either an ignoramus, or is an advocate of the perpetual servility and degradation of his race variety. . . . I believe that two or three millions of us should return to the land of our ancestors, and establish our own nation, civilization, laws, customs, style of manufacture, and not only give the world, like other race varieties, the benefit of our individuality, but build up social conditions peculiarly our own, and cease to be grumblers, chronic complainers and a menace to the white man's country, or the country he claims and is bound to dominate . . . . What the black man needs is a country and surroundings in harmony with his color and with respect for his manhood.

In the early 1890s a few blacks heeded

Bishop Turner's advice and made their way to Mapimi, Mexico, but found life there too hard and returned to their homes in Alabama and Georgia. In 1895, a ship sailed from Savannah, Georgia, for Liberia with 197 blacks aboard. But Liberia at the time was having economic difficulties, the country's citizens were in a state of depression, and the new immigrants encountered many hardships.

For every black who abandoned the South, ten thousand remained there, withstood racism, and succeeded in numerous fields. For every black who was lynched, a skilled worker, a business genius, an inventor or some other talented individual emerged. When white churches barred or segregated black worshippers, when colleges refused to admit black students, when white writers persisted in their false depictions of black life, blacks united and developed their own religious institutions, sought funds to improve their own colleges, and produced their own literature.

For most blacks, gaining education seemed the best way to break through the solid wall of racism that was rapidly building in the South. Thus schools became a first priority, and ways were sought to carry on the work begun by the now defunct Freedmen's Bureau and the Northern religious groups. Fortunately, the period around the turn of the century was one of philanthropy and great interest in education. Wealthy white men were contributing heavily to educational foundations, and by 1900 some 260 institutions

The first Home Office of North Carolina Mutual Life Insurance Company, constructed in 1906.

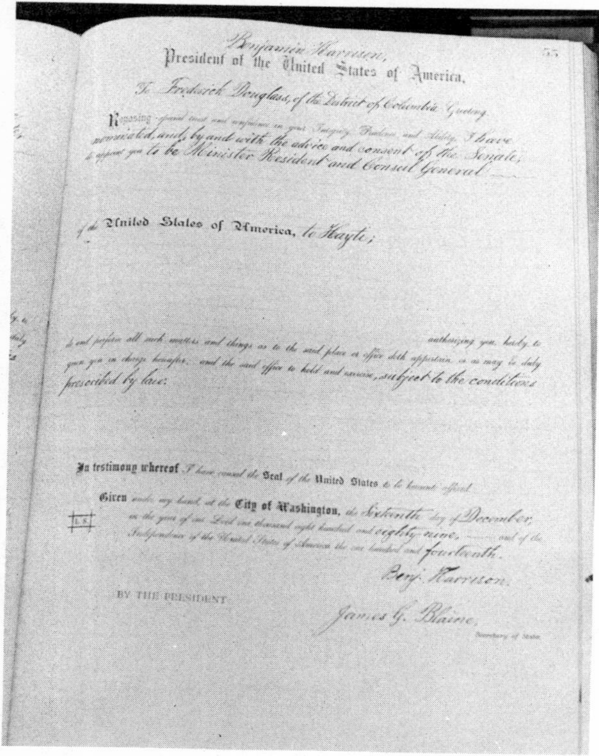

Benjamin Harrison,
President of the United States of America,
To Frederick Douglass, of the District of Columbia, Greeting:
Reposing ... nominated, and, by and with the advice and consent of the Senate, ... to be Minister Resident and Consul General
of the United States of America, to Hayti;
... subject to the conditions prescribed by law:
In testimony whereof ... Seal ... United States ...
Given ... City of Washington, ... Sixteenth day of December, ... eighty-nine, ... fourteenth.
Benj. Harrison.
BY THE PRESIDENT
James G. Blaine,

President Benjamin Harrison's letter appointing Frederick Douglass Minister to Haiti in 1889.

of higher learning had been founded. Most of course, were, for white students—Vanderbilt, Johns Hopkins, the University of Chicago etc.—but blacks reaped benefits from a spillover of concern. Money for the education of black students came from the Peabody Education Fund, the John F. Slater Fund, the General Education Board, the Anna T. Jeanes Fund, the Julius Rosenwald Fund, the Phelps-Stokes Fund and other educational trusts.

It must be pointed out that while white Northerners poured millions of dollars into the black schools of the South, blacks themselves did much to sustain the institutions. Fisk University set an example when its treasurer, George L. White, proposed that the Fisk Jubilee Singers go on a fund-raising concert tour. With money borrowed from teachers and Nashville citizens, the singers journeyed to Oberlin, Ohio, in 1875, to sing at a meeting of the National Council of Congregational Churches. The council was so impressed that it helped spread the word about Fisk's self-help efforts, and within seven years the Jubilee Singers had toured the East and a number of European countries and had raised $150,000 which was used for construction of the university's Jubilee Hall. Success at Fisk led to the sending out of student quartets, choirs, and speakers from other black schools. These personal appearances not only raised funds but encouraged other black youths to seek secondary school and college educations. Thus by 1900 there were 28,560 black teachers and more than one and a half million black children in schools. At the same time thirty-four black colleges were in operation, and state-supported colleges for blacks had been established in Virginia, Arkansas, Georgia, and Delaware. As the nation entered the twentieth century more than two thousand blacks had graduated from colleges and universities, and nearly one thousand were attending college.

While equipping themselves educationally numerous blacks also learned a great deal about competing with whites in the business world. It has already been stated that, in rural areas, thousands of freedmen acquired farm land during and after Reconstruction, and that the growing concentrations of blacks in cities offered opportunities for the development of a number of business enterprises. But during the latter years of the nineteenth century, and continuing until World War I, blacks established innumerable businesses of all types and sizes: grocery stores, drug stores, restaurants, catering firms, bakery shops, tailor shops, building and contract-

Jan E. Matzeliger was the inventor of the lasting machine (right) which revolutionized the shoe-making industry. The machine was patented on March 20, 1883.

ing enterprises, shirt factories, cotton mills, lumber works, carpet factories, rubber goods shops, etc. Cooperative enterprises included the Capitol Trust Company of Jacksonville, Florida; the Bay Shore Hotel Company of Hampton, Virginia; the Southern Stove Hollow-Ware and Foundry of Chattanooga, Tennessee. There were large funeral businesses, a number of insurance companies, and many banks.

It was in banking that blacks made extraordinary strides. As early as 1888, the Savings Bank of the Grand United Order of True Reformers was organized in Richmond, Virginia, by the Reverend W. W. Browne. In the same year the Capital Savings Bank of Washington opened its doors. Then followed the Mutual Bank and Trust Company of Chattanooga, Tennessee, and the Alabama Penny Savings Bank of Bir-

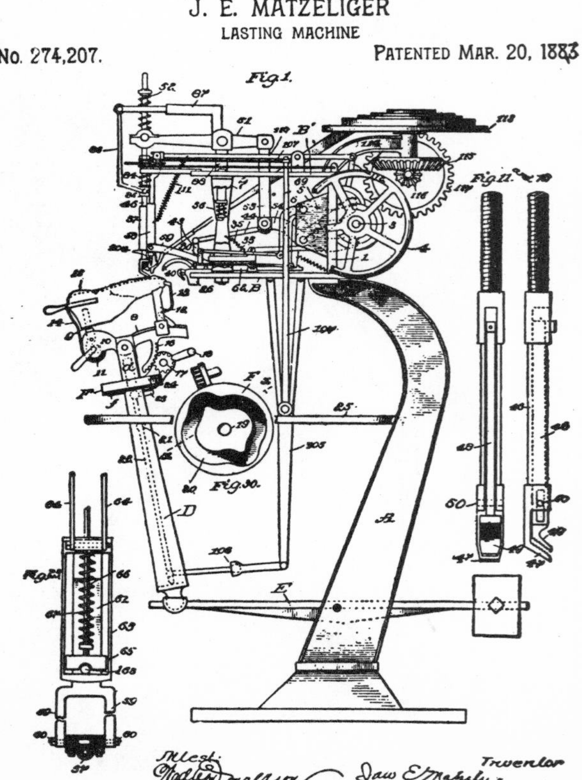

mingham. Within a generation more than fifty banks had been started by blacks. Some lasted only a short while, but others flourished.

Cut off by Jim Crow laws from a variety of cultural institutions and amusement places, blacks devoted themselves to developing their churches, fraternal orders, and various benefit associations. No other institution played as important a role as the church as a place of meeting and fellowship, and as a force for black unity. Although church membership had steadily increased since the very first years of Reconstruction, more enlightened blacks forced the older, conservative denominations to temper their fundamentalist, "pure gospel" ministries with involvement in the myriad problems at hand.

Granville T. Woods, who began inventing in 1885, made significant contributions in the fields of electricity, steam boilers, and automatic air brakes.

To fulfill other needs, blacks relied on such fraternal organizations as the Masons, Odd Fellows, Knights of Pythias, and Knights of Tabor. Early life insurance programs were started in such secret orders as the International Order of Good Samaritans, the Ancient Sons of Israel, the Grand United Order of True Reformers, and the Independent Order of St. Luke. Numerous other organizations avoided secret rituals, special uniforms, etc., and merely provided insurance needs. These organizations collected twenty-five to fifty cents a week from members, and confined their work mainly to single communities, regions, or perhaps a state, as in the case of the four-thousand-member Workers Mutual Aid Associations of Virginia, founded in 1894. It was within these fraternal and benefit organizations that ideas for black life insurance companies grew. One organization, the True Reformers of Washington, lost one of its top men, S. W. Rutherford, when he decided to organize an insurance society which became the National Benefit Life Insurance Company, and which was the largest black insurance organization of its kind well into the twentieth century. In Durham, North Carolina, another worker in the True Reformers, John Merrick, pulled away and led several prominent individuals in organizing a company in 1898 which became the powerful North Carolina Mutual Life Insurance Company. In Atlanta, A. F. Herndon gained control of the Atlanta Mutual Aid Association, and reorganized it into the Atlanta Life Insurance Company.

Black women were not inactive during

the post-Reconstruction period. They were guiding forces behind a number of self-help programs—orphanages, sanitariums, homes for the aged, etc. After its organization in 1895, the National Association of Colored Women began living up to its motto, "Lifting As We Climb," by setting up homes for girls, hospitals, and other agencies. Organized three years earlier, the Colored Women's League of Washington operated a kindergarten and engaged in rescue work. There were few women engaging in business enterprises, but Madame C. J. Walker of Indianapolis developed a line of cosmetics and a method of straightening black women's hair, and became one of America's first woman millionaires.

While blacks had been publishing newspapers for years, none ever achieved the wide circulation and financial success of the *Chicago Defender*, which appeared in 1905 as a handbill edited by Robert S. Abbott. Eventually, blacks across the nation turned to the *Defender* for guidance, and it was a major voice urging blacks to leave the South and migrate to the North. Other outstanding black newspapers of the post-Reconstruction era included the *New Era*, founded in 1870 in Washington, D.C.; the *Progressive American*, a New York weekly which first hit the streets in 1871; *The Philadelphia Tribune* (1884); *The Cleveland Gazette* (1883); the *Savannah* (Ga.) *Tribune* (1885); the *New York*

Dr. Daniel Hale Williams, the pioneer black surgeon, performed the world's first open heart surgery in an early building (opposite page) of Provident Hospital in Chicago.

Age (1887) the Baltimore *Afro-American* (1892); the *Boston Guardian* (1901) and the *Pittsburgh Courier* (1912). These newspapers were the voices of black people—voices which commented on historic, civic, cultural, and social concerns, and voices which called repeatedly for blacks to unite and to use their influence and power wisely and effectively.

Closely allied with the black press were black historians, novelists, and poets of the day. The first major biographer of black individuals was Rev. William J. Simmons, who compiled *Men of Mark: Eminent, Progressive, and Rising* in 1887. Today the illustrated volume is considered a classic of black literature. Histories included George W. Williams's two-volume *History of the Negro Race in America from 1619 to 1880*, which was published in 1883; Edward A. Johnson's *A School History of the Negro Race in America from 1619 to 1890* first appeared in 1891; *History of the Colored Race in America*, which William T. Alexander published in 1888; *Progress of A Race*, by W. H. Crogman (1902); *Primer of Facts Pertaining to the Early Greatness of the African Race*, by Pauline Hopkins (1905) and W. E. B. Du Bois's 1909 book, *Story of the Negro*.

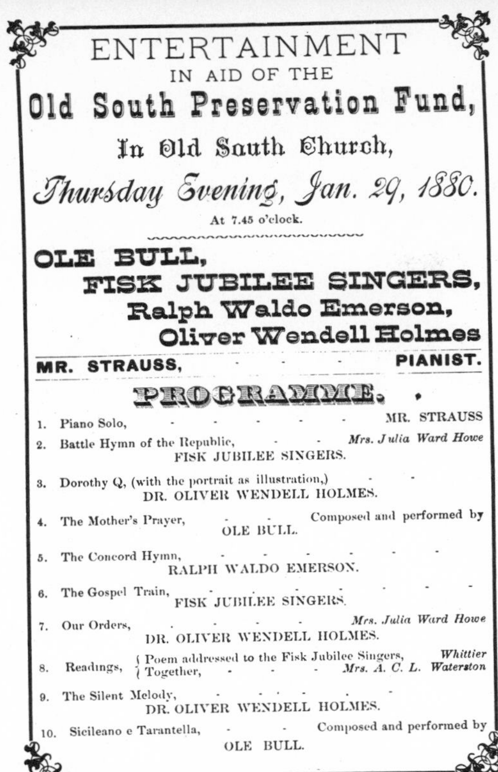

ENTERTAINMENT
IN AID OF THE
Old South Preservation Fund,
In Old South Church,
Thursday Evening, Jan. 29, 1880.
At 7.45 o'clock.

OLE BULL,
FISK JUBILEE SINGERS,
Ralph Waldo Emerson,
Oliver Wendell Holmes

MR. STRAUSS, - - - PIANIST.

PROGRAMME.

1. Piano Solo, - - - - - MR. STRAUSS
2. Battle Hymn of the Republic, - - *Mrs. Julia Ward Howe* FISK JUBILEE SINGERS.
3. Dorothy Q, (with the portrait as illustration,) - DR. OLIVER WENDELL HOLMES.
4. The Mother's Prayer, - - Composed and performed by OLE BULL.
5. The Concord Hymn, - - - - - RALPH WALDO EMERSON.
6. The Gospel Train, FISK JUBILEE SINGERS. - - -
7. Our Orders, - - - - *Mrs. Julia Ward Howe* DR. OLIVER WENDELL HOLMES.
8. Readings, { Poem addressed to the Fisk Jubilee Singers, *Whittier* / Together, - - - - *Mrs. A. C. L. Waterston*
9. The Silent Melody, - - - - - DR. OLIVER WENDELL HOLMES.
10. Sicileano e Tarantella, - - Composed and performed by OLE BULL.

A program and an announcement of a concert by the Fisk Jubilee Singers (opposite page).

PRIVATE MEETING
WITH THE
JUBILEE SINGERS,
Ex-Slave Students from Fisk University, U.S.A.,
AT THE LECTURE HALL,
WOODFORD CONGREGATIONAL CHURCH,
On the Evening of JULY 8th,
AT EIGHT P.M.

CHAIRMAN, ANDREW JOHNSTON, ESQ., J.P.

STEWARDS.
JOSEPH GURNEY BARCLAY, Esq.

E. NORTH BUXTON, Esq., J.P.	Rev. ROBT. MOFFAT, D.D.	JAMES SPICER, Esq., J.P.
SAMUEL ELLIS, Esq.	H. F. BARCLAY, Esq., J.P.	Rev. R. PERCY PELLY, M.A.
WM. FOWLER, Esq., J.P.	Rev. W. H. CHARLESWORTH	ALFRED F. SARGEANT, Esq.
ALFRED TOZER, Esq.	SAMUEL LINDER, Esq.	Rev. SAML. CONWAY, B.A.
Rev. NICHOLAS HURRY	HENRY FOWLER, Esq.	ALEXANDER FRASER, Esq.
Rev. E. T. EGG	THEO. WESTHORP, Esq.	HENRY COOK, Esq.

Admission by Ticket only until five minutes to Eight, when the doors will be thrown open to the public.

Ticket-holders are urgently requested to return their Tickets to Mr. T. FISHER UNWIN, Woodford Bridge, at least two days beforehand if for any reason they decide not to use them.

Subscriptions will be received during the evening, and will go towards the Fund which the Jubilee Singers are raising.

☛ *One or two short Addresses will be delivered during the evening by the*
REV. ROGER PRICE, BAKEREND, SOUTH AFRICA,
and some of the Singers.

THE JUBILEE SINGERS.

SECOND VISIT TO GREAT BRITAIN.

THIS band of ex-slave students from Fisk University, U.S.A., who two years ago made so many friends in Great Britain by their rendering of the weird slave melodies, have returned for a second tour. Additional funds are imperatively needed to complete the furnishing of Jubilee Hall, and to more fully equip the University in other respects for its work. By the violent emancipation of the war, the freed-men of America were left, empty-handed and ignorant, in the midst of their former masters, who were nettled by their enfranchisement and opposed, for the most part, to their education and social elevation. They need Christian sympathy from every quarter, and they need it *now*, before the impulse of the abrupt social changes of the war shall spend its force.

The Singers gratefully remember the cordial welcome they received on their first visit. They hope to be able, now, to meet at least some of the applications for concerts that it was impossible for them to fill before. While five of the old Singers have felt obliged, for varying personal reasons, to retire, these vacancies have been happily filled, and the Company has suffered no loss of strength or distinctive character. They expect to give better concerts than ever before; they hope to make them well worth all they shall cost those who attend them. And their ardent desire is that these little sums, so small singly as to be scarcely felt by those who pay them, may be so large in the aggregate as to make Fisk University not only a great power in the education and elevation of their own people in America, but, through their missionary labours, in the final evangelisation of Africa and the islands of the sea.

THE JUBILEE SINGERS.
EX-SLAVE STUDENTS OF FISK UNIVERSITY, TENNESSEE,
Under the Auspices of THE AMERICAN MISSIONARY ASSOCIATION.

A PRIVATE SERVICE OF SACRED SONG
In the FREE CHURCH, DUNOON,
(REV. MR M'MORRAN'S,)
On THURSDAY EVENING, 21st AUGUST, 1873,
To commence at Half-past Seven.
REV. R. W. THOMSON, CHAIRMAN.

ADMIT THE BEARER.

This Coloured Band appear not as professional singers, but as a Company of Christian Students, desirous of using their musical ability to help their University, which has been built for the higher education of the coloured race. Eight of them are Emancipated slaves, the other three were born free. They have been honoured to sing before the Queen and the Royal Family, as well as in various Halls and Churches in London, and have been received with great enthusiasm.

A Collection will be made during the Service on behalf of the Jubilee Fund, which, it is earnestly hoped, will be liberal.

If this Ticket be not used please return it, as the number issued is limited.

ROBERT M'MORRAN, Free Church, Dunoon.
R. W. THOMSON, U. P. Church, Kirn.
JOHN C. JOHNSTON, U. P. Church, Dunoon.

An admission ticket for a Jubilee Singers concert in Dunoon, Scotland, in 1873.

A strong supporter of these early historians was The American Negro Historical Society, founded in 1897 in Philadelphia. The society collected "relics, literature and historical facts relative to the Negro race, illustrating their progress and development in this country." Another supporter was the Negro Society for Historical Research, founded at about the same time in Yonkers, New York, by John Edward Bruce and Arthur A. Schomburg.

Perhaps the first organization devoted to research in black folk culture was the Society for the Collection of Negro Folklore, which was formed in Boston in 1890. And one of the early voices urging blacks to investigate their heritage was that of H. T. Kealing, editor of *The African Methodist Episcopal Church Review*. As one black writer after another emerged at the turn of the century, he advised them not to imitate white writers but to "explore from the depths of [your] own being where lies unusual materials that is to provide [the black writer] a place among the great writers."

One of the most prolific early black writers was W. E. B. Du Bois, who turned out books, pamphlets, and articles of all kinds, many of them protesting the condition of blacks in the United States. His

Suppression of the African Slave Trade to the United States appeared in 1896 when he was twenty-four, and was the first scientific historical monograph by an American black. It was followed three years later by *The Philadelphia Negro: A Social Study*, written while Du Bois was an assistant instructor in sociology at the University of Pennsylvania. After submitting several articles to such magazines as *Atlantic Monthly*, *Dial*, and *World's Work*, Du Bois then culled his best published and unpublished essays and issued them in a 1903 book titled *The Souls of Black Folk: Essays and Sketches*. The book became an American classic and is still widely read. Not long after publication of the book, Du Bois put all of his savings—about $1,200—into *Moon Illustrated*, a magazine which was intended, he said, as "a high class journal [for] intelligent Negroes." *Moon* never sold more than five hundred copies, and when it failed Du Bois turned to *Horizon*, a magazine he edited until 1910 when he took over editorship of the NAACP journal, *The Crisis*, a magazine which would become one of the most famous in American journalism. Twenty-five years later, while a professor of sociology at Atlantic University, Du Bois completed his monumental, 728-page *Black Reconstruction*.

While the most successful autobiography by a post-Reconstruction black writer was Booker T. Washington's *Up From Slavery* (1900), this work had been

Paul Laurence Dunbar, who died in 1906, was one of the nation's famous men of letters, and the poet laureate of blacks. He wrote several novels during his short life.

preceded by *The Colored Cadet at West Point* (1889) in which Henry Ossian Flipper told of his experiences as one of the first black students at the United States Military Academy, and by *The Life and Times of Frederick Douglass,* a fascinating autobiography which first appeared in 1881 and was updated and enlarged eleven years later. In 1899, four years after Douglass's death, Charles W. Chesnutt's *Frederick Douglass* appeared. Chesnutt followed this biography with a number of novels and short stories and became one of the major writers of his era. His works include: *The Conjure Woman, The House Behind the Cedars, The Marrow of Tradition,* and *The Colonel's Dream.*

Often described as the "poet laureate" of the black race was Paul Laurence Dunbar, who emerged in the early 1890s as a gifted interpreter of black life. As a hotel elevator operator he wrote verse and submitted several examples to daily newspapers and magazines. Soon he was being compared with Whittier, Longfellow, and Lowell. Though Dunbar lived only thirty-four years, his output included numerous poems (among the most famous: "When Malindy Sings," "When de Co'n Pone's Hot," "The Party" and "The Poet and His Song") and several novels, including *The Uncalled* (1898) and *The Love of Landry* (1900).

A contemporary of Dunbar was black artist Henry Ossawa Tanner, whose paint-

Charles W. Chesnutt, a novelist and short story writer.

George W. Williams, a soldier and historian.

ings won medals at the Paris Exposition of 1900, the Pan-American Exposition of 1901, and the St. Louis Exposition of 1904. Tanner was acclaimed as one of the world's great artists at the turn of the century, and his work hangs in art museums in both the United States and Europe. One of the era's most important organizations of black intellectuals was the American Negro Academy, whose purpose was, "the promotion of literature, science and art . . . the fostering of higher education, the publication of scholarly work and the defense of the Negro against vicious assault." The latter phrase was indicative of the involvement of blacks at all levels in racial problems of the late nineteenth century.

The academy's organizer and first president was the Reverend Alexander Crummell, who had studied the classics and theology at Cambridge University in England.

Henry Ossawa Tanner, an outstanding painter at the turn of the century.

Tanner's large output of paintings included (opposite page) *The Annunciation*, *The Thankful Poor*, and (right) *Abraham's Oak*.

In medicine, the most distinguished post-Reconstruction physician was Dr. Daniel Hale Williams, a graduate of Chicago Medical College. Dr. Williams entered private practice in Chicago and later helped in the founding of the city's Provident Hospital, the first interracial hospital in the United States. It was there that he gained international fame as the first surgeon to operate successfully on the human heart.

In post-Reconstruction music and theater the best known names were those of J. Rosamond Johnson, James A. Bland, Will Marion Cook, Sisseretta Jones, Bob Cole, George Walker, and Bert Williams.

Johnson was famous as the composer of such songs as "Under the Bamboo Tree" "Oh, Didn't He Ramble" and "Lazy Moon," and wrote the music for "Lift Every Voice and Sing," a poem composed by his brother, James Weldon Johnson. The song became known as "The Negro National Anthem," and has been sung in black churches and schools and at meetings of black organizations for generations.

Bert Williams was a famous theatrical performer, both on the West Coast and on Broadway.

Lift Every Voice And Sing

Lift ev'ry voice and sing
Till earth and heaven ring,
Ring with the harmonies of
Liberty;
Let our rejoicing rise
High as the list'ning skies,
Let it resound loud as the rolling seas;
Sing a song full of the faith that the
dark past has taught us,
Sing a song full of the hope that the
present has brought us;
Facing the rising sun
Of our new day begun,
Let us march on till victory is won.

Stony the road we trod,
Bitter the chast'ning rod
Felt in the days when hope had died;
Yet, with a steady beat,
Have not our weary feet
Come to the place for which our
fathers sighed,
We have come over a way that with
tears has been watered,
We have come, treading our path
thro' the blood of the
slaughtered,
Out from the gloomy past,
Till now we stand at last
Where the white gleam of our bright
star is cast.

God of our weary years,

James Bland composed perhaps seven hundred songs, many of which are well-known.

Will Marion Cook was a major black composer.

God of our silent tears,
Thou who hast brought us thus far on the way;
Thou who hast by Thy might,
Led us into the light.
Keep us forever in the path, we pray,
Lest our feet stray from the places, our God, where we meet Thee,
Lest, our hearts drunk with the wine of the world, we forget Thee,
Shadowed beneath Thy hand,
May we forever stand,
True to our God, true to our Native Land.

James Bland performed in minstrel shows in the United States and in England (where he lived for nearly twenty years as a famous star), and is said to have written about seven hundred songs, but only thirty-eight were copyrighted in Washington. His most famous tunes were "Oh, Dem Golden Slippers," "In the Evening by the Moonlight," and "Carry Me Back to Old Virginny," which the Virginia House of Delegates adopted in 1940 as the official state song.

Bland had no formal musical training, but Will Cook studied under Anton Dvorak, and in 1898 composed a one-act musical, *Clorindy—The Origin of the Cakewalk*, which became a New York theater "hit." In later years, Cook composed a number of Broadway scores.

These Frederic Remington drawings depict black troopers and cavalrymen of the West. At left, *A Halt to Feed.* Below, *The Dough Boys on the March.* Opposite page, *Captain Dodge's Troopers to the Rescue.*

The most famous musical team of the era was Williams and Walker, two young men—George Walker was from Kansas; Bert Williams was from Antigua in the West Indies—who sang and danced their way from California to the East in 1896 and became successful in music halls. With Williams as a burnt-cork comedian and Walker as a well-dressed "straight man," they appeared in *The Song of Ham,* a musical farce that ran for two years. Even more popular was their *In Dahomey,* with music by Cook, lyrics by Paul Laurence Dunbar, and book by Jess Shipp. The show opened in 1902, then went to London where the royal family ordered a command performance in Buckingham Palace. The team had enjoyed stardom for only ten years when Walker died. Williams continued as a star in otherwise all-white Broadway productions and later signed a long-term contract to appear with the famous Ziegfeld Follies.

In another area—sports—blacks also excelled. At the turn of the century three names were well known: Peter Jackson, Isaac Murphy, and Marshall W. ("Major") Taylor. Jackson was a heavyweight boxer hailed as the "Black Prince of the Ring," and made the same kind of ring history which was later recorded by Jack Johnson, Henry Armstrong, and Joe Louis. Murphy, perhaps the greatest of all black jockeys, rode three Kentucky Derby winners in the 1880s. In the unusual sport (for blacks) of bicycle racing, Taylor was the American sprint champion in 1898 when he was twenty years old. Until his retirement twelve years later he held the title, "The Fastest Bicycle Rider in the World." Long before World War I, blacks were frozen out of both professional horse-racing and bicycle-racing, but continued winning titles in the boxing ring.

Post-Reconstruction era blacks also distinguished themselves as inventors of numerous useful devices. The United States Patent Office has no accurate records of the race of early patent applicants, and it is not known how many blacks contributed their inventive genius to America's industrial growth. But it is believed that at least fifteen hundred inventions were registered by blacks between Reconstruction and World War I. Among the more famous black inventors of that time were Jan E. Matzeliger, a black Dutch Guianan who, in 1883, patented a shoe lasting machine which was purchased by the United Shoe Machinery Company of Boston, and which effectively reduced the cost of shoe manufacturing by more than 50 percent; Granville T. Woods, who began work about 1885 on inventions ranging from electronics to steam boilers and automatic air brakes,

Booker T. Washington was born in 1863 in a Virginia slave cabin. After working in West Virginia salt mines, he taught school in an old church, then opened Tuskegee Institute in 1881.

and whose various inventions in the field of telegraphy were bought by the American Bell Telephone Company, the General Electric Company, and the Westinghouse Air Brake Company before his death in 1910; John J. Parker, who in 1884 set up his own foundry and machine company to manufacture a screw for tobacco presses which he had invented; and Elijah J. McCoy, who in 1872 patented an automatic lubricating device which became widely used on railroad trains and steamships. In addition to the lubricating device, a number of his other inventions were used in industrial plants.

Among the most significant actions by blacks after Reconstruction ended were moves in the direction of an all-black political party. One such move was the formation in 1883 of the Colored Independent party by a group of Pennsylvanians under the leadership of William Still and

Robert Purvis. Blacks both North and South felt cut off from meaningful political participation in either major party. Not even Frederick Douglass, a loyal Republican, objected. "Follow no party blindly," was his advice. "If the Republican Party cannot stand a demand for justice and fair play, it ought to go down."

In Massachusetts, black Judge George L. Ruffin formed the Massachusetts Colored League in 1885, denounced the Republican party, and suggested that blacks withdraw their support of a party which had turned its back on black rights and demands. One other voice which urged black political independence was that of Timothy Thomas Fortune, editor of the influential *New York Age*. "Give us a new party," he demanded while denouncing "the infamous barter and treachery—the effeminate, the juvenile, the nerveless policy pursued by Mr. R. B. Hayes."

What actually emerged during the 1880s was not a strong all-black political party but an adventure in Populism, an alliance with poor whites of the South who had become dissatisfied because of the changed interests of the Democrat ruling class. The Southern wing of the Democratic party was being taken over by industrialists and merchants, men with whom the small farmer had few common interests, and men the farmers blamed for the deteriorating economic conditions that had resulted in the Panic of 1873. Thousands of farmers had lost their land in an agricultural depression, and now

An informal portrait of Booker T. Washington, a dominant personality among blacks until his death in 1915. His last home is shown below.

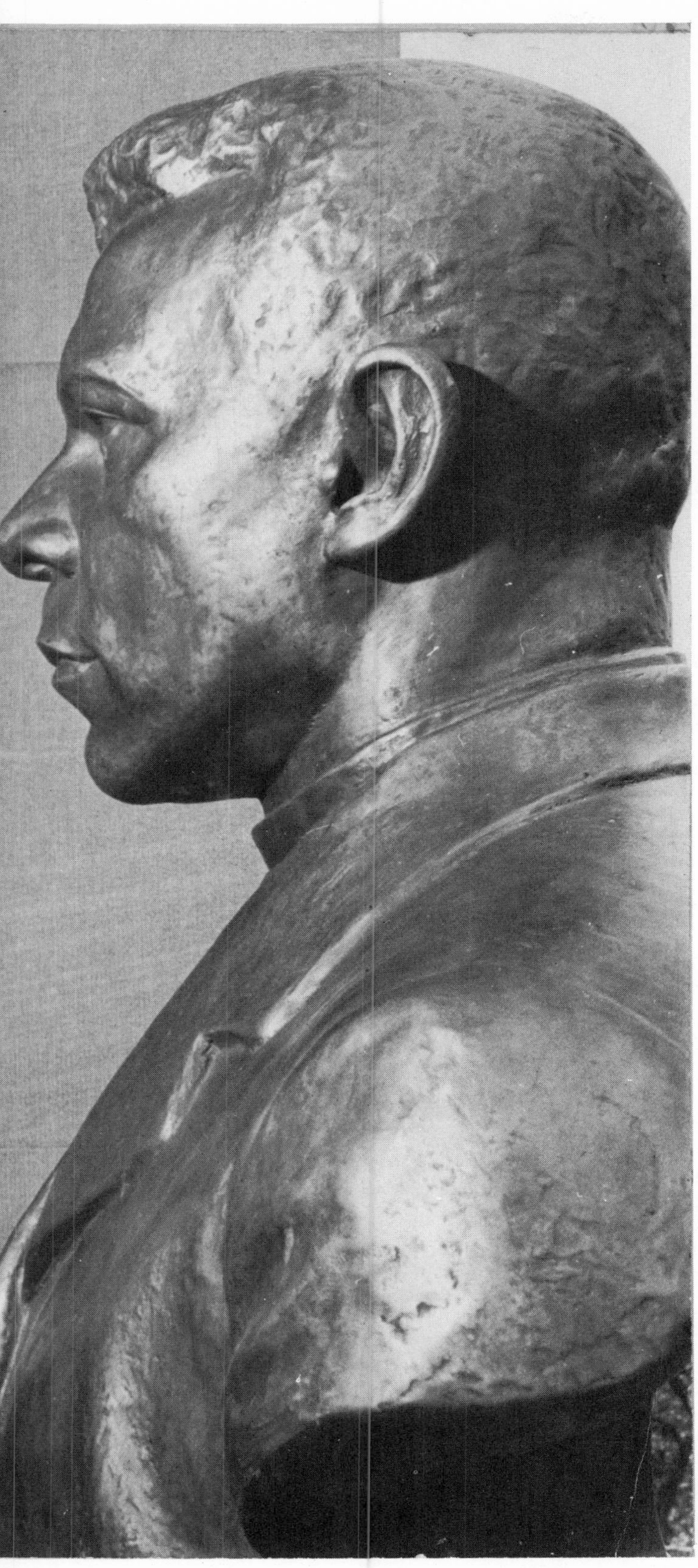

they turned in fury against the monied Democrats who had foreclosed mortgages, the Democratic state governments that steadily raised taxes, and the railroad lines that charged ever higher freight rates while receiving subsidies from state and federal taxes. The impoverished whites were willing, for a time, to lay aside considerations of race and join with blacks in a coalition searching for avenues to a better life. The all-white Southern Farmers' Alliance, which had some three million members, and branches in every Southern state, urged blacks to form a parallel organization. Thus in 1886 the Colored Farmers' National Alliance was organized in Houston County, Texas. Within five years it claimed more than one million members with local chapters all over the South. The SFA and CNFA cooperated closely, listening to radical agrarian leaders such as Tom Watson of Georgia, who preached that blacks and whites were being deliberately kept apart by Democrats afraid of the power that the two groups could wield.

The black and white farmer groups met together for the first time in 1890 in Ocala, Florida, to map strategy for action. Newspapers across the South headlined news of the integrated convention.

But third party activity was delayed. Instead, the two groups formed various cooperatives and exchanges for joint purchase of seeds and equipment, and for the sale of crops. (Blacks had such exchanges in Houston, New Orleans, Mobile,

This bust of Booker T. Washington by black sculptor Richmond Barthé stands in the Hall of Fame at New York University.

Charleston, and Norfolk.) And in the 1890 election they supported only those Democrats who pledged themselves to a political platform that had been written at the Ocala convention. After the election, the alliances claimed control of eight state legislatures, four governors, forty-four congressmen, and a senator.

With fourteen hundred members in attendance, and by now joined by labor representatives, the alliances met for the second time on May 19, 1891, in Cincinnati. Whereas a year before they had faced a desperate struggle and needed all the black support they could get, Southern delegates had won major victories and now could flex their muscles—and expose their racism. They tried to segregate blacks by

William Monroe Trotter, editor of *The Guardian*, was a fiery spokesman demanding black rights.

THE GUARDIAN.

VOL. I. NO 44. BOSTON, MASS., SATURDAY, SEPTEMBER 6, 1902. PRICE 5 CENTS

THEY SLIPPED ROGERS AWAY.

Brockton Officers Took the Prisoner Off While Under a Habeas Corpus

THE EDUCATION OF THE NEGRO.

DIED IN LIFE'S BLOOM.

BARRED BY WHITES.

DRAW COLOR LINE.

The *Guardian* was founded by Monroe Trotter in 1901.

The founders of the Niagara movement included W. E. B. Du Bois (2nd row, c.).

proposing separate meetings, but the proposal was voted down. They also split with blacks on the third party issue: black delegates supported the idea, while Southern whites preferred a takeover of the Democratic party. Despite the differences, the two groups emerged from the convention agreeing on political unity if not social equality. The Populist movement spread and white Democrats were caught up in panic. They made overtures to Populists and were rebuffed. Then, in desperation, they turned to the blacks they had disfranchised and intimidated into staying away from the polls for a decade. Now blacks were begged—and often forced—to vote.

While black politicians—this time Populist ones—were once again subjected to intimidation and terror (some fifteen were killed during the Georgia state elections in 1892, and there were riots in Virginia and North Carolina), many blacks stuck by the Populists, and in some areas there was a fusion between the new party and the remnants of the old Republican party. In 1894 such a fusion of voters seized the North Carolina legislature and threw the state's Democrat machinery into disarray. In a resurgence of black political power—especially in the Black Belt eastern section of the state—by 1895 hundreds of blacks were elected as magistrates, deputy sheriffs, policemen, and aldermen. There was a similar resurgence in Georgia and in other parts of the South

South Carolina in 1890, now was an outspoken racist and worked actively to pass a bill requiring segregation on railroad cars. And Tom Watson, whom blacks had come to regard as such a true friend and savior that they rushed to touch his hand whenever he appeared in public, now joined those Southern whites involved in the plan to disfranchise blacks through the literacy test and "grandfather clause."

By the late 1890s the white Populists had been completely absorbed by the Democratic party, and the Democrats tried to ensure that blacks and whites would never again be able to coalesce and pose a threat. One by one, "Jim Crow" segregation laws were put into effect: separate eating and drinking places, separate railroad cars, separate drinking fountains, separate toilets, "black" and "white" textbooks for schools—separate everything. South Carolina even forbade black and white cotton mill workers to look out of the same window. Later, Oklahoma would require "Colored" and "White" telephone booths, New Orleans would segregate black and white prosti-

These Spanish-American war pictures show members of the Twenty-fifth Infantry (below) and black soldiers loading a transport ship at Tampa, Florida (top, right). The Hotchkiss Battery is shown in action at Las Guasimas, Cuba.

though on a more limited scale.

The rebirth of black political power lasted only as long as 1896. By then the agrarian revolt had collapsed and poor whites had settled back into their racist ways, convinced in their ignorance that the South once again faced "black rule." Fears, prejudices, and old hatreds had combined to heal the split in white ranks. The "Solid South" was solid again. "Pitchfork Ben" Tillman, who had appeared "liberal" enough to win sufficient black votes to become the Populist governor of

tutes, and Atlanta courts would have separate Bibles on which witnesses took oaths.

Legal sanction for the raft of Jim Crow laws came in 1896 from the U. S. Supreme Court in the *Plessy* vs. *Ferguson* decision, establishing the "separate but equal" doctrine which would remain in effect until May 17, 1954. Homer Plessy was a man who considered himself seven-eighths white and only one-eighth black. He had gone to court charging that a Louisiana law, requiring segregation on trains within the state, violated his rights under the Thirteenth and Fourteenth amendments. The crux of Plessy's case was a warning that if a physical distinction—skin color, for example—could be used as a basis for segregation, then discrimination against persons with blond or red hair could also be considered reasonable and legal. And Plessy argued that, in legally sanctioning segregation of some of its citizens, Louisiana implied that such citizens were inferior in the eyes of law.

The Court, in an eight-to-one decision, ruled that segregation by race did not necessarily imply racial inferiority. *Plessy* was reduced to a "question of whether the statute of Louisiana [is] a reasonable regulation," and the Court held that for a state legislature to act in conformity with "established usages, customs, and traditions of a people . . . and the preservation of the public peace and good order," was, in fact, "reasonable."

Once again, as he had been thirteen years earlier in the decision on the Civil Rights Cases of 1883, Associate Justice John Marshall Harlan was the lone dissenter. He wrote: "In the view of the Constitution . . . there is in this country no superior, dominant, ruling class of citizens. There is no caste here. Our Constitution is color-blind. In respect of civil rights, all citizens are equal before the law." But *Plessy* vs. *Ferguson* stood as the South's legal guidepost for more than half a century.

The year before the *Plessy* decision, one of the most prominent black men in the nation took a position which almost everyone interpreted as approval of the philosophy of racial segregation.

It was September 18, 1895, and Booker T. Washington, a former slave who had built Tuskegee Institute in Alabama and served as its president, a man whose "soundness" on racial matters had made him a leader of white opinion with a national following, a man who had taken over as the new leader of the black race after the death on February 20, 1895, of

Frederick Douglass, had been invited to Atlanta to address the opening day audience of the Cotton States and International Exposition. James Creelman, a famous correspondent of the *New York World*, described the appearance of Washington that day "... a remarkable figure; tall, bony, straight as a Sioux chief, high forehead, straight nose, heavy jaws, and strong, determined mouth, with big white teeth, piercing eyes, and a commanding manner. The sinews stood out on his bronze neck, and his muscular right arm swung high in the air, with a lead-pencil grasped in the clenched brown fist. His big feet were planted squarely, with the heels together and the toes turned out. His voice rang out clear and true, and he paused impressively as he made each point. Within ten minutes, the multitude was in an uproar of enthusiasm—handkerchiefs were waved, canes were flourished, hats were tossed in the air. The fairest women of Georgia stood up and cheered."

Washington began his speech with a disarming concession: "I was born in the South and I understand thoroughly the prejudices, the customs, the traditions of the South. I love the South." Whites cheered, and they cheered more when he

George H. White of North Carolina was the last black man to sit in Congress in the post-Reconstruction period. His congressional term ended in 1901.

said that he had learned that "these prejudices are something that it does not pay to disturb," and that "the agitation of questions of social equality is the extremest folly." He reminded white Southerners of the "fidelity and love" of blacks during the Civil War, and thanked "those Christ-like philanthropists," the wealthy whites of the North, who were helping him provide industrial education for his students. Then he began speaking in metaphors about empty buckets and open hands.

> A ship lost at sea for many days [he said] suddenly sighted a friendly vessel. From the mast of the unfortunate vessel was seen a signal, "Water, water; we die of thirst!" The answer from the friendly vessel at once came back, "Cast down your bucket where you are." A second time the signal, "Water, water; send us water!" ran up from the distressed vessel, and was answered, "Cast down your bucket where you are." A third and fourth signal for water was answered, "Cast down your bucket where you are." The captain of the distressed vessel, at last heeding the injunction, cast down his bucket, and it came up full of fresh, sparkling water from the mouth of the Amazon River. To those of my race who depend on bettering their condition in a foreign land or who underestimate the importance of cultivating friendly relations with the southern white man, who is their next-door neighbor, I would say: "Cast down your bucket where you are . . ."

To whites in the audience, Washington offered the same advice.

> Cast down your bucket . . . among the eight millions of Negroes . . . who have, without strikes and labor wars, tilled your fields, cleared your forests, builded your railroads and cities . . . the most patient, faithful, law-abiding, and unresentful people that the world has seen.

With cheers ringing in his ears, Wash-

Dr. Mary Church Terrell (l.) was a famous educator and fought all her life for black rights. Madame C. J. Walker was America's first black woman millionaire, while Mrs. Ida B. Wells Barnett (extreme right) was a militant antilynching spokesman.

BUFFALO LAGER
Johnson Club

ington suddenly flung his hand aloft with the fingers spread apart.

In all things that are purely social, [he shouted], we can be as separate as the fingers, yet [he balled the fingers into a fist] one as the hand in all things essential to mutual progress.

In his dispatches, reporter Creelman wrote that "a great wave of sound dashed itself against the wall, and the whole audience was on its feet in a delirium of applause."

When the applause had subsided, Washington said:

The wisest among my race understand that the agitation of questions of social equality is the extremest folly, and that progress in the enjoyment of all the privileges that will come to us must be the result of severe and constant struggle rather than of artificial forcing.

Jack Johnson was one of the greatest of all heavyweight boxing champions.

The speech ended and again whites cheered. What about the blacks in the audience? Reporter Creelman wrote a prophetically chilling sentence: "Most of the Negroes in the audience were crying, perhaps without knowing just why."

The speech became known immediately as "the Atlanta Compromise;" it made Washington famous and set the tone for black leadership for nearly a quarter-century. At one of the worst moments in black history, Washington undertook the task of conciliating racist whites and serving as mediator between them and aroused black people. He felt that his mission was to preach a gospel of conservatism, patience, and material progress, and to build Tuskegee Institute into the best institution offering industrial education that would not antagonize Southern whites and that would, at the same time, prepare black youngsters for the types of work that would be offered them in the South. Instead of a program of classical education, Washington's Tuskegee Institute offered courses that prepared blacks to be farmers, mechanics, domestic servants, and the like. While he did not discourage the study of history, science, and mathematics, such subjects were, in his opinion, impractical at the time. He believed that "for years to come the education of the people of my race should be so directed that the greatest proportion of the mental strength of the masses will be brought to bear upon the everyday practical things of life, upon something that is needed to be done, and something which they will be permitted to do in the community in which they reside." Washington won white friends for his school in both North and South and Tuskegee developed into one of the South's best institutions of its type.

Later, it would be revealed that Booker T. Washington had personally financed some of the earliest court cases against segregation. He apparently hoped that eventually blacks would win complete acceptance by whites and be integrated into American life. "I would set no limits to the attainments of the Negro in

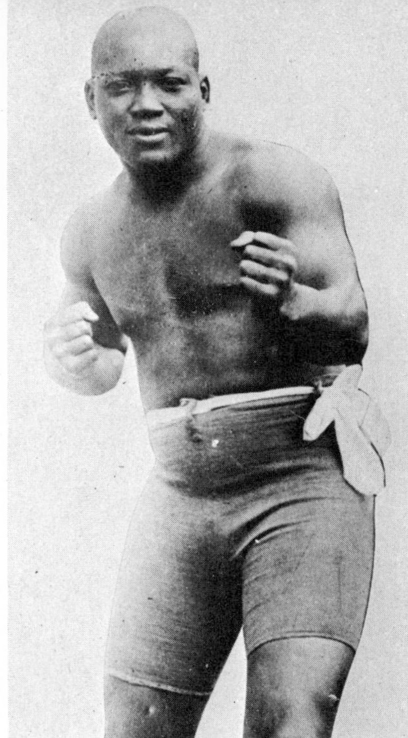

Jack Johnson in a fighting pose and (below) with boxer Stanley Ketchel (left) and ring czar "Sunny Jim" Coffroth. Opposite page shows Johnson in action, and (bottom) Harry Wills, one of the most masterful boxers of all times.

arts, in letters or statesmanship," he said on one occasion, "but I believe the surest way to reach those ends is by laying the foundation in the little things of life that lie immediately about one's door. I plead for industrial education and development for the Negro not because I want to cramp him, but because I want to free him. I want to see him enter the all-powerful business and commercial world."

Naturally, Washington's ideas and his ever growing prestige as the spokesman for millions of blacks made him the object of criticism from blacks of more progressive mind. His foremost critic was William E. B. Du Bois, a young black man who had studied at Fisk, Harvard (where he had earned the Ph.D. degree), and Berlin. Du Bois was a Northerner from Massachusetts, but his concern for black students had brought him to Atlanta University as one of its most learned professors. A master of research techniques, he had amassed

The *Afro-American* Newspapers Building in Baltimore, Maryland, the headquarters for one of the nation's largest black newspapers.

T. Thomas Fortune, editor of the *New York Age.*

Robert L. Vann, editor of the *Pittsburgh Courier.*

Robert S. Abbott, editor of the *Chicago Defender.*

John H. Murphy Sr., editor of the *Afro-American.*

a wealth of information about the condition of blacks in the South. As far as he was concerned, the educational program advocated by Washington was too narrow and too predominantly economic in its objectives. Washington preached "a gospel of Work and Money to such an extent as apparently almost completely to overshadow the higher aims of life," he wrote.

On the matter of Washington's extending "an olive branch" to racist Southern whites, Du Bois was particularly cutting. It was he who dubbed Washington's Atlanta speech the "Atlanta Compromise."

While Du Bois never relented in his criticism, Washington remained the nation's most powerful black man—a friend of wealthy and powerful white men, a counselor of U. S. presidents, a dispenser of political patronage—until his death in 1915. But meanwhile, Washington's famous "bucket" was delivering year after year of misery for blacks, South and North. During the educator's later years, white mobs made lynchings, burning of black homes and businesses, and terrorizing blacks a part of "the American way of life." From 1900 until the year of Wash-

W. E. B. Du Bois (c.) with employes in the editorial office of *The Crisis.*

Mary White Ovington and Arthur B. Spingarn were among the leaders of the NAACP from 1909–10.

ington's death, 1,267 blacks were lynched, according to records at the educator's own Tuskegee Institute.

The constant wave of terror, and Washington's inability to persuade either his influential white friends or his government contacts to move effectively against the perpetrators, contributed to the calling together of a group of blacks by Du Bois in 1905. Du Bois felt the need to launch his own movement, a call went out, and about thirty blacks from thirteen states and the District of Columbia met at Niagara Falls, Canada. (Hotels on the New York side refused to accept them.) While they avoided open criticism of Washington, the conference participants issued a manifesto calling for freedom of speech and of the press, an end to race and color discrimination, and recognition of the principles of human brotherhood. Mention of "freedom of speech" and "freedom of the press" in the manifesto was actually a slap at Washington, who had become so powerful that few black newspapers dared oppose him editorially. What the black men—educators, editors, professionals—who gathered around Du Bois intended, they announced, was (1) to oppose firmly the present methods of strangling honest criticism, manipulating public opinion and centralizing political power by means of the improper and corrupt use of money and influence; (2) to organize thoroughly the intelligent and honest Negroes throughout the United States for the purpose of insisting on manhood rights, industrial opportunity and spiritual freedom, and (3) to establish and support proper organs of news and public opinion.

What the Niagara movement intended was aggressive action, thus Du Bois and the others were promptly branded as "preachers of radicalism." Despite open attacks on their program, they met the following year at Harpers Ferry, Virginia, site of the martyrdom of John Brown, with more than one hundred persons in attendance. A number of resolutions—which Du Bois said he had written in "a tumult of emotion"—were presented at this second conference.

After Harpers Ferry, annual meetings of the movement were held at historic freedom spots, and some thirty branches were formed. But Du Bois never won the support of the black masses, and by 1910 the Niagara movement quietly ceased its operations. Some said that Booker T. Washington had worked behind the scenes to destroy it. Nevertheless, it was the Niagara movement which was the forerunner of the National Association for the Advancement of Colored People, an organization in which Du Bois played a major role.

The NAACP was organized on the cen-

W. E. B. Du Bois is shown at work on one of the issues of *The Crisis*, which first appeared in 1910.

tennial of the birth of Abraham Lincoln, February 12, 1909, in New York City, mainly by liberal whites who gathered to protest a riot in Springfield, Illinois. The group was called together by Oswald Garrison Villard, the grandson of abolitionist William Lloyd Garrison, for a "discussion of present evils, the voicing of protests and political liberty." Among Villard's supporters were Du Bois, Mary White Ovington, Jane Addams, Francis J. Grimke, Bishop Alexander Walters and William Dean Howells. Absent was one of Du Bois's old friends and supporters, the fiery editor William Monroe Trotter, who sent word that he no longer trusted "white folks."

A year after its founding meeting, the NAACP opened offices in New York with Moorfield Storey, a white Boston lawyer and former secretary to Senator Charles Sumner, as president, and Du Bois (who resigned from his teaching position at Atlanta University) as director of publicity and research, and editor of the organization's official organ, *The Crisis*. A number of distinguished white attorneys—including Clarence Darrow, Louis Marshall, and Felix Frankfurter, who later went to the U. S. Supreme Court—served without charge on the NAACP's first legal redress committee and filed a number of lawsuits challenging Jim Crow laws. The first vic-

THE CRISIS

A RECORD OF THE DARKER RACES

Volume One NOVEMBER, 1910 Number One

Edited by W. E. BURGHARDT DU BOIS, with the co-operation of Oswald Garrison Villard, J. Max Barber, Charles Edward Russell, Kelly Miller, W. S. Braithwaite and M. D. Maclean.

CONTENTS

PUBLISHED MONTHLY BY THE

National Association for the Advancement of Colored People

AT TWENTY VESEY STREET NEW YORK CITY

ONE DOLLAR A YEAR TEN CENTS A COPY

tory was in 1915 when the Supreme Court nullified the "Grandfather clauses" in the Maryland and Oklahoma state constitutions as violations of the Fifteenth Amendment. By 1921 the NAACP had more than four hundred branches.

An organization that somewhat paralleled the NAACP in purpose and growth was the National Urban League, which grew out of a "Committee on Urban Conditions among Negroes" formed in 1910 by George Edmund Haynes, a young black graduate student in social work at Columbia University, and Mrs. William H. Baldwin Jr., a white woman who had worked in the League for the Protection of Colored Women. The Urban League announced that its purpose would be the improve-

Mrs. William H. (Ruth Standish) Baldwin was a cofounder of the National Urban League. Edwin R. Seligman was the first chairman of the League's Board.

ment of conditions of blacks in cities and that it would be especially interested in increasing employment opportunities. Booker T. Washington decided to join a group of sponsors of the new organization which included such wealthy whites as Julius Rosenwald. The Urban League also established headquarters in New York and organized a number of branches. Cornell University graduate Eugene Kinkle Jones was appointed executive secretary in 1914, and in 1921 the sociologist Charles S. Johnson became director of research and investigation. Two years later he founded the League's magazine, *Opportunity, A Journal of Negro Life,* whose slogan was "Not Alms, but Opportunity."

Both the NAACP and the Urban League settled into their work at what was another crucial time for blacks. In 1913 Woodrow Wilson entered the White House as the first Southern Democrat president since the Civil War. Against a background of continued intimidation and lynching of blacks, half of the new president's cabinet were Southerners, and his first Congress was flooded with racist, antiblack legislation—more than had ever been introduced at a single session. Blacks had little to look forward to from Wilson—and especially from continued residence in the South—when the presi-

Dr. George E. Haynes (top photo) and Eugene Kinckle Jones were the first executive officers of the National Urban League, founded as the National League on Urban Conditions among Negroes.

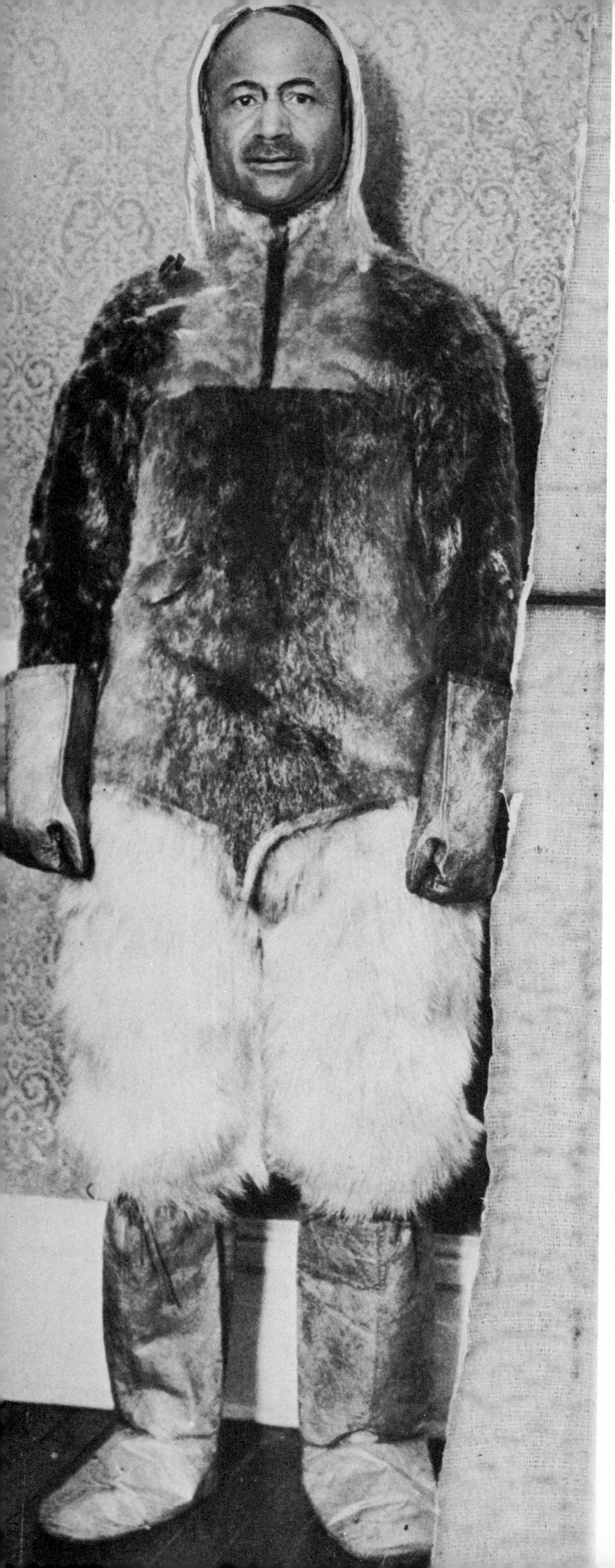

Matt Henson in the clothes he wore during his polar expedition with Admiral Robert E. Peary. The first American to reach the Pole, Henson is shown (top photo) with the Eskimos who were with him.

dent himself issued special orders segregating almost all black federal employes in Washington. Another sign of the times was the reactivation of the Ku Klux Klan —this time beneath a fiery cross on Stone Mountain near Atlanta, and for the unprecedented amount of racist venom which poured from such Southern Democrat Senators as J. Thomas Heflin of Alabama and James Vardaman of Mississippi. Among Vardaman's pronouncements: "I am just as opposed to Booker Washington as a voter, with all his Anglo-Saxon reenforcements, as I am to the coconut-headed, chocolate-colored, typical little coon, Andy Dotson, who blacks my shoes every morning. Neither is fit to perform the supreme function of citizenship."

Heeding the advice of the *Chicago Defender* that it was "better to die of frostbite than at the hands of a mob in the South," many thousands of blacks packed their few belongings and began a trek to the North.

3

Migration

Some are coming on the passenger,
Some are coming on the freight,
Others will be found walking,
For none will have time to wait.

This poem was one that black men, women, and children remembered and recited all through the South during the first decades of the new century. White Southerners were infuriated by black schoolboys chanting the words sing-song fashion, and sheriffs arrested black men caught with copies of the *Chicago Defender* in which the poem appeared. "Inciting to riot" was the usual charge, and

the penalty was a term at a prison farm. But nothing could stop what would become a legend: The Great Northern Drive—the departure from the South of blacks by the tens of thousands, all heading to the *Defender*'s Chicago and to Cleveland, St. Louis, Indianapolis, New York . . . anywhere across the Mason-Dixon line.

Mail poured into the *Defender* office. A New Orleans black woman wrote:

> Please sir, will you kindly tell me what is meant by the Great Northern Drive to take place May 15, on Tuesday. It is a rumor all over town to be ready for the 15th of May to go in the drive . . . Do please write at once and tell me of this excursion to leave the South. Nearly the whole of the South is ready for the drive. Please write at once. We are sick to get out of the South.

Another woman wrote:

> I reads your paper and I am asking about the drive of May the 15. We want more understanding about it for there is a great many of us that wants to come and the depot agent never gives us any satisfaction when we ask for they don't want us to leave. Please put in your paper Saturday, just what time the train will be here, and the fare so we can be there on time. Many women are wanting to come. They are hard-working women, the white folks tell us we have to have plenty of money to come north, if this is right let us know, also let us know where the train is going to stop.

From 1900 to 1920 the black population of New York City increased by ninety-one thousand; of Chicago by seventy-nine thousand; of Philadelphia by seventy-three thousand, and of Detroit by thirty-six thousand. It is estimated that similar increases in other cities added at least five hundred thousand blacks to Northern city populations during the first twenty years of the century.

This movement of blacks from South to North was not without precedent. There had been the "Exodus of 1879," and there had been a steady flow of blacks into Northern areas since the days of the "Underground Railroad." By 1900, 911,025 blacks were living in the North, 10.3 percent of the nation's 8,883,994 blacks. But there had been nothing to match the number of individuals and families caught up in the Great Northern Drive.

A number of factors combined to produce the phenomenon. There was, of course, the usual amount of racism—

which not even a rash of widely heralded black heroism had helped ease. A black American, Matthew Alexander Henson of Washington, D. C., had been the first man to reach the North Pole, and black soldiers had distinguished themselves in both the Spanish-American and Mexican Wars, and in skirmishes with Indian tribes. None of this had mattered; the Southern way of intimidation, lynching, and burn-

Often entire families gave up plantation life for the promise of better things in the North.

ing had persisted. Indeed, the viciousness of the acts had increased. There were the retrograde steps of President Wilson's administration; and there had been a natural disaster which had disrupted plantation life: a swarm of boll weevils had swept through the South, devastating cotton crops. Crops missed by the boll weevils had been destroyed by a series of storms and floods. Black sharecroppers and plantation workers, who had been earning no more than forty cents to $1.75 a day, now had either to leave the South or starve. Opportunity was in the North. The war in Europe had cut off the flow of immigrant labor to America, and the nation's involvement in that war was draining away thousands of job-age men. Thus to the *Chicago Defender*'s appeals ("Why should the Negro stay in the South?" asked editor Robert S. Abbott. "It is true the South is nice and warm, and may I add, so is China, and we find Chinamen living in the North, East and West") were added those of Northern job recruiters for defense plants, shipyards, steel mills, and packing houses. Fanning through the South, these recruiters painted glowing pictures of conditions "up North," and helped organize blacks into clubs which then secured special travel rates, especially on the Illinois Central Railroad. Chicago-bound "specials" began rolling from town to town in the South, wherever the Illinois Central had tracks, and blacks packed not only the passenger coaches but also the special freight cars that were added one by one. "Farewell—We're Good and Gone" and "Bound for the Promised Land" and "Bound to the Land of Hope" were among the slogans chalked on the sides of the trains by the happy "exodusters," as the departing blacks were called. Within a period of eighteen months in 1917–18, an estimated fifty thousand blacks arrived in Chicago, according to daily counts made at the Illinois Central depot.

The migration left huge labor gaps in the Southern industries dependent upon black workers. Thousands of acres of rice and sugar cane rotted in the fields because of a shortage of harvesters. The turpentine industry of North and South Carolina and the milling industry in Tennessee were hard-pressed. Cotton growers in the Mississippi Delta began making concessions of various kinds to black workers. The situation became so critical that the South's entire economic structure was threatened. The whites began organizing. They began a whisper campaign of lies concerning "17,000 Negroes counted in the bread lines of Chicago." Stories of numerous

A typical plantation cabin in the rural South.

blacks "freezing to death in the North's horrible winters" were widely circulated. Daily newspapers in both the North and South conspired to create a new image of the South and promote its "change of heart" in racial matters. "Louisiana Wants Negroes to Return," was a headline in the *Chicago Tribune*. Banner headlines in the Washington *Post* included this one: "South Needs Negroes. Try to Get Labor for Their Cotton Fields. Tell of Kind Treatment." In the Philadelphia *Press:* "South Is Urging Negroes to Return. Many Districts Willing to Pay Fare of Those Who Come Back." And in the Memphis *Commercial Appeal:* "South Is Best for the Negro, Say Mississippians. Colored People Found Prosperous and Happy." Other efforts by desperate whites including the hiring of black "leaders" to denounce the migration and urge blacks not to "go off way up yonder where the icicles hang down big as trees, and where the white folks you don't even know." A particularly vicious effort by whites in some states was that of falsely arresting droves of black men, charging them with minor offenses, and imposing fines which could not be paid. Thus the men were forced to remain in the state. Those who slipped away were often seized and brought back under extradition laws. The *Defender* reported one such case:

Southern kidnappers made a bold and successful raid on Chicago citizenship Saturday when in broad daylight a sheriff from Mississippi went to the railroad yards at Eighteenth Street and with the help of Chicago police "captured" a man named James Halley, and in less than two hours had this man handcuffed and on a train bound for Holly Springs, Mississippi, to stand trial for selling a pint of whisky, made a penitentiary offense for the purpose of establishing a new form of slavery in the South and setting forth a complicated condition of affairs in the state which the Race has started to fight in order to protect its own citizens from illegal kidnaping.

Not only was selling whisky an offense. There were reports of Southern lawmen coming north to arrest black men on numerous charges of "insulting a white woman," and an Atlanta detective actually collared a black man on a Chicago street and informed him that he was wanted back home for "spitting on the sidewalk."

Since it had played such a major role in setting off the migration, the *Defender* undertook the responsibility, in Chicago, of advising the newcomers of their rights and of assisting them with legal help. The newspaper ran this notice:

ATTENTION NEWCOMERS
If the police attempt to molest you and you
are not guilty, or if you get in trouble,
send for one of the following lawyers.
F. L. BARNETT-184 W. Washington Street
ELLIS and WESTBROOKE-3000 South State Street

And the newspaper offered advice: "Quit calling the foreman "boss." Leave that word dropped in the Ohio River. Also captain, general, and major. We call people up here Mister This and Mister That." Also, "When you get among white workmen, treat them as you want them to treat you—AS A MAN—not as an inferior . . . There is no law that requires you to tip your hat to a man because he is white."

Once settled in Northern cities, blacks began enjoying many of the privileges that had been denied them in the South. There was, of course, no formal segregation in amusement places and on street cars, and once again blacks could vote as they pleased. As a result, they elected

Black churches provided spiritual relief from the nightmare of terror against blacks seeking their constitutional rights.

Oscar De Priest to the Chicago City Council in 1915. Two years later, Edward A. Johnson of New York City won a seat in the New York state assembly. Black votes were so important in such cities as Chicago, New York, Cleveland, Cincinnati, and Philadelphia, that the political parties in power had to win black favor or face defeat. Thus blacks began appearing in elective offices in these towns and won a small number of appointive posts.

But all was not pleasant. Though the Urban League tried desperately to open doors of employment to the newcomers, white resistance forced some highly qualified blacks into menial jobs. (It must be remembered that, while 70 percent of the black population of the South was rural, many skilled workers and some professionals had joined the Northern exodus.)

In addition to job problems, there were riots in such cities as Chester, Pennsylvania, Youngstown, Ohio, and East St. Louis, Illinois, precipitated by white laborers who were afraid that black workers would lower wages or completely take away their jobs. At East St. Louis, in July, 1917, a white mob with guns drove blacks into a congested black neighborhood, set houses on fire and massacred 125 black men, women, and children. East St. Louis (which had become one-third black) had long been a hotbed of racial hostility, and in the courts blacks received worse punishment than the whites who started the riot. One black man was brought to trial and sentenced to life imprisonment but was later freed. Ten black men were sentenced to ten years in prison, but only four white men were given fourteen- to fifteen-year sentences. Five other whites served five years, eleven served less than one year, eighteen were fined, and seventeen were set free.

During the years of World War I, competition for jobs and housing caused racial hostility to simmer throughout the North. Although the American Federation of Labor was forced, by the sheer number of black workers, to admit blacks to membership, the white rank and file of the unions—many of them European immigrants who had arrived just before the outbreak of war—deeply resented having to work beside a black man. This resentment spilled over into neighborhoods, and white homeowners began fleeing as soon as a black family bought a house in the same block. Thus the rise of the urban ghettos which plague almost every Northern city even today.

There was so much hostility during the last six months of 1919—there were more than twenty race riots—that black poet James Weldon Johnson described those months as "The Red Summer," the redness being the blood of blacks and whites that was spilled on the nation's streets.

After the riots, Southern employers renewed their efforts to entice black workers back "home," but relatively few returned.

A black family arrives in Chicago from the rural South.

Young black migrant workers moved from job to job in the early 1900s, riding on freight trains.

4

World War I

BLACK AMERICANS, their horizons structured by the tremendous problems facing them in the United States, cared little about what was going on in the rest of the world as the second decade of the twentieth century began. While there was a stirring of interest in Africa, brought on mainly by the activities and writings of such men as Henry McNeal Turner and W. E. B. Du Bois and the preaching of Marcus Garvey, who started his back-to-Africa movement in the West Indies in 1914, the masses of blacks thought in terms of "up North" and "down South." Schools for blacks in the South were few and poorly staffed and those in the North were not much better. It is little wonder that blacks had little concern for the power struggle which had been brewing in Europe and which was soon to explode into World War I, a conflict that was to involve them more than any previous war.

Woodrow Wilson, a Southerner and a Democrat, was elected president in 1912, and while he had the reputation of being a liberal, black Americans soon found out that his "liberality" had nothing to do with the rights of minorities. In fact, during his first Congress more than twenty bills attempting to restrict the rights of blacks were introduced. Luckily most of them were defeated. Wilson himself, through an executive order, Jim-Crowed the federal civil service by setting up separate lunchrooms and washrooms.

Throughout the South, the boll weevil was wreaking havoc on the cotton crops; and the cotton farmer—wealthy plantation owner and the poor tenant farmer or sharecropper—faced economic disaster.

Understandably, blacks paid little attention to newspapers whose headlines screamed that on June 28, 1914, Archduke Francis Ferdinand and his wife Sophie had been assassinated. A black man feeding a family of six in a fourth-floor walkup flat in Harlem on less than fifteen dollars a week had more important things to think of than what was going to happen in Europe because the heir to the throne of Austria-Hungary had been killed by a Bosnian student who had once lived in Serbia. A sharecropper in Mississippi watching his few acres of cotton being devoured by boll weevils knew little and cared less about the issues that had driven European rulers to the brink of war.

From huge posters, a stern Uncle Sam pointed his finger at every passerby. "Uncle Sam Wants YOU!" the posters proclaimed. The finger pointed impartially at black and white citizens and, along with their patriotic white brothers, black men flocked to recruitment offices to sign up.

The whites who volunteered were taken into the services but most blacks were rejected. It was plain to most black leaders that in one way this "war to make the world safe for democracy" was no different from earlier United States wars—black men would have to fight for their right to fight.

Black men were turned away from recruiting stations during the first month of the war. They were refused primarily because the military leaders did not know what to do with them. The regular army had some ten thousand black men on its roster. These men were the members of the Ninth and Tenth Cavalry regiments and the Twenty-fourth and Twenty-fifth Infantry regiments. These four regiments were the only major black units in the army. Black National Guard units had an additional ten thousand members, giving black America some twenty thousand soldiers in uniform at the beginning of the war.

Once the vacancies in these units were filled, the army had no place to send its black recruits. This problem was complicated even further when, on May 18, the government passed the Selective Service Act which ordered the registration of every able-bodied male from twenty-one to thirty-one years of age. The government was still thinking white but more than seven thousand blacks registered on July 5 and the big problem was thrown into the lap of the military.

The army had no confidence in black soldiers as combat troops, and would have been very happy to put them all in the Services of Supply (SOS) where they could serve as laborers, stevedores, bakers,

Muffled drums were the only sound as this NAACP-sponsored silent march protested wartime lynchings.

A conference of black editors was held in Washington, D.C., to discuss treatment of black soldiers.

truck drivers, gravediggers, etc. This doubt persisted although there was sufficient evidence from the performance of black combat men in the Revolution, the War of 1812, the Civil War, and the Spanish-American War to prove otherwise.

The fledgling NAACP supported a campaign to have the government set up an officers' training camp for black men. It was indicative of the thinking in Washington that General Leonard Wood told Joel Spingarn of the NAACP that a training camp would be set up *if* he could locate two hundred Negroes of college grade who wanted to be officers.

The lone black officers' training camp (there were fourteen organized for whites) began operation in June, 1917, at Fort Des Moines, Iowa, with some 1,250 men enrolled. In October, 639 black officers were commissioned: 106 captains, 329 first lieutenants, and 204 second lieutenants.

While the Fort Des Moines school turned out the majority of black officers for World War I, it was by no means the only source of commissioned men. Black men from the regular army and National Guard units who qualified for officers' training were sent to Camp Hancock in Augusta, Georgia, for machine gun officers' school, to the infantry officers' training school at Camp Pike near Little Rock, Arkansas, or to artillery officers' training school at Camp Taylor near Louisville, Kentucky. At these schools, the black men were quartered separately but were trained with white officers.

In all, more than twelve hundred black officers served in World War I. The best-known of them, however, never saw action in France. This was Lieutenant Colonel Charles Young, the third black man to graduate from West Point and the only black West Pointer in the military at the beginning of the war.

Young was "retired" from the army on July 30, 1917, with the rank of colonel. His forced retirement brought a flood of criticism from black leaders throughout the country. As a matter of fact, Colonel Young was forced into retirement because his rank and seniority qualified him to lead a regiment. As a regimental commander, he would have had white officers under his jurisdiction and there were many who could not abide this thought. Colonel Young's background was interesting. He was graduated from West Point in 1889 and was at first assigned to the Tenth Cavalry Regiment and then reassigned to the Twenty-fifth Infantry Regiment before he could report. The young second lieutenant protested that he was a cavalry man and that he had already ordered cavalry uniforms at a great deal of expense. He was then transferred to the Ninth Cavalry Regiment over the protests of the white commanding officer who did not want another black officer, even though he had a vacancy. He took Young only on the promise that he would be transferred to the Tenth Cavalry at the first opportunity.

Colonel Young was an unusual man for an army officer—white or black. He wrote plays and poetry and composed music and yet was a hard-working military man devoted to duty. His skill and diplomacy was so respected by the government that he was sent to assist black governments in

Emmett J. Scott was special assistant to the secretary of war.

both Haiti and Liberia as a military expert. When Young returned to the United States after contracting a severe case of malaria in Liberia the president of that country wrote the United States government praising the black officer for the services he had rendered.

In 1916, Young was serving in Mexico under General John J. Pershing (later to command all U.S. troops in Europe) who then recommended Young as an officer fit to command militia. Former President Theodore Roosevelt, whose Rough Riders are said to have been saved by the Ninth and Tenth Cavalry regiments in Cuba during the Spanish-American War, said during one speech that Colonel Charles Young was one black officer "fit for the extraordinarily difficult task" of commanding an Army regiment.

But the government officials (some say the decision came from President Wilson himself) decided that Young would be retired and the word was released that he had high blood pressure. Despite the fact that his private doctor said that Young's blood pressure was normal for a man of his age and that Young dramatized his fitness by riding horseback from his home in Chilicothe, Ohio, to Washington, D.C., the army retirement board refused his request and retired him.

Civilians drafted under the Selective Service Act report for training at cantonment.

Colonel Young was brought out of retirement and served for a brief time at Camp Grant in Illinois in 1918. After the war he was returned to Liberia as a military expert. He contracted malaria there for the second time and died in 1922.

Although the black officers' training camp at Fort Des Moines, Iowa, was the only training facility set up specifically for the training of black troops, black enlisted men were trained at regular military posts throughout the nation. Training was done on a segregated basis, and most of the officers and non-commissioned officers involved were white.

Black men as well as white men were swayed by the patriotic fervor that gripped the nation. But for some time it seemed that they would not be allowed to show their fighting skills. The majority of blacks were assigned to service units where they were to set records for moving vast quantities of supplies and the rapid loading and unloading of ships.

Black leaders and organizations continued to press for full use of black men in the military—particularly the army. The marines had no black members at all and intended to stay white. The navy, once well integrated but now almost entirely white, would take only a handful of Negroes and these primarily as messmen and menials. *The Crisis*, the publication of the NAACP, edited by fiery young W. E. Burghardt Du Bois, campaigned for black officers and combat troops. German propagandists spread the word that the United States would not grant democracy to its black citizens.

Criticism of the government reached such a level that President Wilson had Secretary of War Newton D. Baker name a black man as special assistant and confidential advisor on black affairs. The man chosen was Emmett J. Scott, a brilliant man, for eighteen years confidential secretary to black leader Booker T. Washington, who had died in 1915. Some black leaders felt that Scott, like the man for whom he had so long labored, was too much of a gradualist to do an honest job for black people. Scott's job was to advise the War Department on how it should treat black soldiers and he was also to help build better morale among black troops already in the service. The job was a thankless one. Just a month before his appointment, the soldiers of the Twenty-fourth Infantry Regiment had rioted against the white citizens of Houston, Texas, because of the stringent Jim Crow practices in the city and the brutal treatment a policemen had given a soldier who refused to observe them. Before the riot ended, seventeen whites had been killed and many others wounded. Rapidly brought to trial, thirteen of the men involved in the riot were sentenced to death and summarily hanged. Life sentences were meted out to forty-one others and an additional forty were held for further investigation.

Scott turned out to be an indefatigable worker and his office handled thousands of complaints of discrimination—many of them against Selective Service boards accused of not giving fair and equal treatment to black men who reported for draft hearings.

Scott's office also helped establish a Students' Army Training Corps and vocational detachments in some twenty black schools and colleges. Several black universities were later awarded Reserve Officers' Training Corps (ROTC) departments for the training of black officers.

But despite these steps, black leaders continued to demand a combat division, and the War Department finally activated the Ninety-second Division. Made up of the 365th, 366th, 367th and 368th in-

During a break at Camp Travis, Texas, soldiers enjoy a boxing bout sponsored by the YMCA.

fantry regiments and the 350th and 351st machine gun battalions, the Ninety-second included other necessary divisional troops such as artillery, engineers, signal, service, and headquarters.

The Ninety-second was commanded by white General Charles C. Ballou, the officer who had commanded the black officers' training camp at Fort Des Moines. The division first trained together at Bourbonne-les-Bains in northeastern France just sixty miles south of the battle front. Two months after arriving in France, the Ninety-second took over defense of its first sector of the battle line at St. Die.

While the Ninety-second was the first black U.S. division to see service as a unit overseas, it was neither the first black unit to serve in France nor the first to face fire. The first black troops to join the American Expeditionary Force abroad were members of a stevedore battalion which reached France in June, 1917. The first U.S. black combat troops to see action were members of the 369th Infantry Regiment which was attached to a French division and went into action in May, 1918.

But the Americans were Johnny-come-latelies in combat so far as black troops were concerned. From the beginning, black troops in the French army—most of them from Senegal and the Sudan—had distinguished themselves at the front.

The 369th Infantry Regiment was a part of the Ninety-third Infantry Division—an abbreviated black division made up largely of regiments from some eight National Guard units. In fact, the Ninety-third Division never really materialized as an actual division. The 369th, 370th, 371st and 372nd Infantry regiments were sent to France as the nucleus of the Ninety-third Division but they were attached to the French army and served overseas under the command of the French. The 369th (formerly the Fifteenth New York National Guard Regiment) earned the French Croix de Guerre for its gallantry in action in a battle which began at Maison-en-Champagne. In addition to the unit citation, some 171 men and officers of the 369th were individually honored with the Croix de Guerre or the Legion of Merit. The 369th was also the first unit of the Allied armies to reach the Rhine River.

The Eighth Illinois National Guard Regiment, made up primarily of black men from the Chicago area, became the 370th U.S. Infantry Regiment and made history as the only regiment of the U.S. Army to be called into service with an almost complete complement of black officers—both commissioned and noncommissioned. Colonel Franklin A. Denison commanded the regiment with distinction in the states and abroad.

The 370th sailed to France and after six weeks of training with French arms and equipment under French instructors, the regiment was attached to the Tenth Division of the French Army on June 11, 1918.

Colonel Charles Young was a West Point graduate who served in the cavalry.

On June 21, the 370th occupied the then-quiet St. Mihiel sector of the front. In early July the men were transferred to the Argonne Forest, then a relatively quiet sector, although the 370th sustained its first casualty there, a private from Chicago, named, ironically, Robert E. Lee.

By mid-September, the regiment was in the Soissons sector and took part in the battles leading up to the capture of Mont des Signes, an exceptionally strong German position. Sergeant Matthew Jenkins of the 370th earned both the American Distinguished Service Cross and the French Croix de Guerre.

The 371st and 372nd Infantry regiments were units made up of National Guardsmen and draftees. The 371st was organized at Camp Jackson, South Carolina, on August 31, 1917, with all white officers.

The 372nd Infantry Regiment was composed of National Guard units from Washington, D.C., Ohio, Massachusetts, Connecticut, and Maryland, and draftees from Michigan and Wisconsin.

Both the 371st and 372nd regiments were attached to the 157th Division, the famous "Red Hand" division of the French Army.

The 371st saw its first action near Verdun and then took part in the Champagne offensive. The men of the 371st earned fame for the accuracy of their weapons fire when they shot down three German planes during their advance near Monthois. Casualties for the 371st during the Champagne offensive were staggering. Of 2,384 men engaged in action between September 28 and October 6, some one thousand were killed or wounded. The performance of the black troops in this offensive won the regiment commendation from the French Army and 146 individual citations.

When the Ninety-second Division took over the St. Die sector from the American Sixth Infantry Division, the Sixth had recently captured the village of Frapelle and the Germans were determined to recapture it. Thus the members of the Ninety-second found themselves immediately under fire. Skirmishes between patrols and artillery duels occurred daily and five days after taking over the sector, the Ninety-second repulsed a German attempt to retake Frapelle.

The Ninety-second occupied the St. Die sector from August 25 until September 20 and during that time captured their first prisoners, five Germans taken by a raiding party from the 366th Infantry. It was during this period, too, that the division lost its first prisoners when two black soldiers were captured by the Germans, who launched a propaganda attack aimed at the black troops. The Germans fired shells containing leaflets into the American position. The leaflets were addressed to "the colored soldiers of the American Army" and questioned why black soldiers were fighting for democracy.

Black officers as well as enlisted men served with honor in World War I.

Some of the many black officers of the 368th Infantry Regiment.

The Ninety-second Division left the St. Die sector on September 21 and was transferred to the Argonne where some 650,000 American soldiers were to join the Allies in the last great thrust of World War I against the Hindenburg Line.

When the Ninety-second first moved into the Meuse-Argonne offensive, both the 365th and the 366th infantry regiments were pressed into duty building roads across "no man's land" under almost constant fire. The regiment was next transferred to the Marbache sector. By the middle of October, the soldiers of the Ninety-second had crossed the Moselle River and were driving the enemy back. They were in full command of the sector when the Armistice was signed on November 11, 1918. The First Battalion of the 367th Infantry received a unit citation of the Croix de Guerre for its bravery on November 10 and 11 in the drive to Metz.

Shortly before the Ninety-second Division was to return to the United States, the troops were reviewed and commended at LeMans by General John J. Pershing, commander-in-chief of the American Expedition Forces.

General Pershing was not the only officer with high praise for black troops. French generals Garnier Duplessis and Mariano Goybet were unstinting in their praise of the regiments of the Ninety-second Division.

But all was not sweetness and light for the black combat and supply soldiers either at home or overseas. In fact, it was racial tension between the black New Yorkers of the Fifteenth National Guard Regiment and white South Carolinians in Spartansburg that led to the regiment's being shipped so quickly abroad. The Fifteenth (it became the famed 369th) was shipped to Camp Wadsworth with the white New York National Guard units for training before being shipped overseas. Both the white officers of the Fifteenth and white civilian leaders of Spartanburg feared trouble. (The regiment went to South Carolina just two months after the riot in Houston.) For a moment it looked as if they were right. According to Major Arthur D. Little, a battalion commander with the 369th, soldiers of the Fifteenth heard that two "colored soldiers" had gotten into a fight with the police and had been hanged in the yard of the police headquarters. It turned out that two members of the Fifteenth were missing from reveille that same morning. Quietly, a group of some forty black soldiers got rifles and ammunition and marched into town to check on the story. Marching in uniform and in perfect order, they aroused no suspicion. Their officers caught up with them as they waited "at ease" on the street while two of their members went to check with police about the two missing men. The police had no record of the men and the rumor was soon proved false. The officers quietly marched the men back to camp and white

Among black women who took part in war work were Mary E. Belcher (top, l.), Mrs. Alice Dunbar Nelson, widow of poet Paul Laurence Dunbar (top, r.), Eva D. Bowles (center), Mary E. Jackson (lower, l.), and Mrs. Louise J. Ross (lower, r.).

Spartanburg never realized how close they had come to a riot, for the men admitted that if the story had been true they were prepared to shoot up the entire town.

Similar conflicts occurred all over the American South. In 1917, thirty-eight blacks lost their lives to lynch mobs and in 1918 the number rose to fifty-eight. In East St. Louis, Illinois, a riot started when a factory started hiring black workers and some forty blacks were killed.

Despite the reports of discrimination and the acknowledged segregation in the armed forces, black men flocked to the recruiting offices and the Selective Service places of registration. Before the war ended some 2,300,000 black men and 21,500,000 whites had registered for the draft. Of the black men who registered, 51.67 percent were put in Class A (eligible for service) while only 32.53 percent of the whites were so classified. From June 1, 1917, through the end of the war, 16 percent of the black men who registered were drafted, against only 11 percent of whites.

By the war's end, some four hundred thousand black volunteers and draftees were in the armed forces and some one hundred thousand served in France. There were three hundred eighty thousand blacks assigned to the Services of Supply branch of the army and eighty thousand of these men were sent overseas, primarily to unload ships, drive trucks, build railroads and do other manual labor. Nearly all of the approximately twenty thousand black troops assigned to combat were sent to the front as part of the Ninety-second or Ninety-third divisions.

A vigilant black press of some five hundred weekly newspapers, including such stalwarts as the *Chicago Defender*, the *Cleveland Advocate*, the *New York Age* and the Baltimore *Afro-American*, kept black civilians aware of what was happening to the black soldier in the United States but its coverage of the soldier overseas was limited. The papers could not afford to send correspondents abroad and had to rely on the meager black news released by the War Department, the occasional story by a white correspondent, or the not too reliable and usually censored letters from soldiers themselves. Blacks protested vigorously against the ignoring of activities of black troops and finally, just two months before the war's end, the government appointed a black correspondent, Ralph Tyler, to cover the activities of black troops abroad.

Tyler's appointment grew out of a request at a conference which Scott held with thirty-one leading black newspapermen in June, 1918. The newspapermen also denounced mob violence, asked that Colonel Charles Young be returned to active duty, and requested that black Red Cross nurses be used.

One of the few black publications which refused to support the nation's war effort wholeheartedly was the *Messenger*, a New York newspaper published by A. Philip Randolph and Chandler Owen. The editors were sentenced to two and a half years in jail and denied second-class mailing privileges after publishing an article entitled "Pro-Germanism Among Negroes."

Most black people supported the war. Despite the fact that they earned less than any other ethnic group, black people purchased more than $250 million in Liberty Bonds and War Stamps. As individuals, and as members of church and civic groups, schools and businesses, blacks pledged their money to help "make the world safe for democracy." The North Carolina Mutual Life Insurance Company bought three hundred thousand dollars' worth of Liberty Bonds in less than two years.

The Committee on Public Information of the federal government, a public relations body for the War Department, was charged with preserving citizen morale—especially the morale of groups with "special grievances." Upon the suggestion of Scott, the Committee on Public Information appointed a "Committee of One Hundred"—one hundred black ministers, editors, educators, businessmen, fraternal heads, etc., who served as emissaries of the government in spreading patriotism and keeping up morale among black folk.

Like their black brothers in the armed forces and on the home front, black women desired to participate fully in the war effort. But, like black men, they encountered obstacles. The first organization to which most women turned was the American Red Cross, an organization in which some eight million women worked during World War I. How many of these were black is not known, for the Red Cross claimed that it "enlisted workers without regard to race, creed or color and no separate records were maintained of the work of any particular Auxiliary." In most cities in the North, black women were recruited to work with whites, but in some Northern and all Southern cities, separate black auxiliaries were organized under white jurisdiction. In many cities, black women were not allowed to work at the soldiers' canteens.

Association. The War Work Council was founded to aid young women who went to towns near army camps to be close to their husbands, brothers, or friends. The War Work councils set up centers where couples could meet, and established Hostess Houses where the women could stay in comfort and safety. The War Work Council assigned $400,000 of its 1918 budget to finance work among black women.

American Red Cross workers (opposite page) provided canteen services to all black troop trains passing through Chicago. The group above maintained a YWCA Hostess House at Camp Upton on Long Island, N.Y.

The Nursing Division of the Red Cross was responsible for recruiting nurses for service in military hospitals, but until June, 1918, black nurses were not authorized for service. Hundreds who had registered with the Red Cross were then dispatched to camps where black troops were quartered.

Black women found a great deal of satisfaction in working for the War Work Council of the Young Women's Christian The War Work Council eventually included one black national secretary, twelve national workers, three field supervisors and forty-two centers with sixty-three paid workers. The Council also opened fifteen Hostess Houses with complete staffs of black women.

The Industrial Section of the War Work Council, under the direction of Mary E. Jackson, concentrated on aiding the working women who left their homes for war work in the plants of urban centers. Black women in the Women's Division of the Council of National Defense worked on the registration of women, the weighing and measuring of babies, the establishment of milk stations, health and recreation stations, the supervision of women in industry, child welfare, and food conservation. The War Camp Community Service helped enlisted men who were away from home and organized chaperoned dances at the Community Service Clubs.

The National Association of Colored Women worked diligently in relief and bond drives. The NACW's membership grew to one hundred thousand, and helped black women raise some $5 million during the Third Liberty Loan campaign, according to Mrs. Mary B. Talbert, its 1918 president.

While women did yeoman work on the home front, it was a male organization, the Young Men's Christian Association, which served black soldiers at the military camps and abroad. The War Work Council of the YMCA had promised to provide the same services for black and white troops. Dr. J. E. Moorland, YMCA senior secretary in charge of colored men's work, headed a staff which included Robert B. DeFrantz, William Faulkner, Max Yergan, Charles H. Wesley, J. Francis Gregory, and George L. Johnson.

The War Work Council had decided to send only black secretaries to the fifty-five centers in army camps where black troops were quartered. Located in National Guard buildings, barracks, mess halls, or tents, these YMCA centers were staffed by some 268 secretaries. An additional forty-nine secretaries served overseas. The centers provided religious services, athletics, educational classes, movies, dances, and other social events for the soldiers. The YMCA also taught thousands of soldiers how to read and write.

There was a great deal of criticism of the YMCA policy of segregation. Black men were excluded from church services in Southern camps that had no separate black YMCA center. White canteens throughout the South refused to serve black soldiers, and black soldiers were unwelcome at YMCA entertainment sessions both in the states and abroad.

The YMCA sent sixty-eight black men and nineteen black women overseas during the war. Among these were Max Yergan, who had already done excellent work with black British troops in Africa; John Hope, president of Morehouse College, and Dr. H. H. Proctor, pastor of the First Congregational Church in Atlanta, Georgia. These men served mainly in areas where there was racial friction, disciplinary problems, or other difficulties.

The war wrought a tremendous change in the lives of millions of black Americans. For the black soldiers there were, naturally, many changes, including, for some, crippling injuries and even death. At the least, the black soldier faced an extended

A Saturday night dance in Baltimore gave troops a break in training.

time away from his family and job (both of which were sometimes gone when he returned home) and a change in attitude —especially if he had served some time in the relatively raceless culture of France.

World War I had changed the American economy on the home front also, and it was never to be quite the same again. The war in Europe cut off the flow of white immigrants who had been filling the new jobs opened in factories, mines, and mills.

Another four million men were taken out of the labor pool and put into the U. S. Army. The government itself hired thousands of additional employes, and industry now had to increase its tempo to take care of the war needs of the United States and its allies. Suddenly, Northern industry discovered the black man and woman. At the same time blacks were leaving the

South in protest against living conditions.

The South fought back with threats to blacks and Northern agents. But the threats did not prove effective. From 1916 through 1918 it was estimated that more than a million blacks fled the South.

Since black men were in short supply, industry wooed the black woman. Black women became truck drivers, auto mechanics, switchboard operators, elevator operators, ditch diggers, and airplane plant workers.

The labor shortage emancipated more black people than Abraham Lincoln and, as the war drew to a close, labor and industry knew that things could never be the same again. The secretary of labor, viewing the vast change in black employment, established a Division of Negro Economics and appointed Dr. George E. Haynes, a cofounder of the Urban League and a professor of social sciences at Fisk University, its director.

Industry and labor had discovered the black worker and next in line was the labor union. Black laborers, so long ignored or kept out by labor unions, now found the unions taking a second look. Recognizing the handwriting on the wall, some labor unions decided they should accept blacks into full membership but some blacks declined the invitation. The American Federation of Labor, resolving to bring black labor into the fold, held a conference on black labor. Among those invited were Dr. R. R. Moton, principal of Tuskegee Institute; Emmett Scott, special assistant to the secretary of war; George W. Harris, editor of the *New York News;* A. H. Grimke, president of the Washington branch of the NAACP; E. K. Jones, executive secretary of the Urban League; John Shillady, secretary of the NAACP, and Fred R. Moore, editor of the *New York Age*. The black leaders emphasized the necessity of removing all barriers preventing blacks from entering the highly skilled trades. They urged the AFL to organize blacks in the various trades, North and South, men and women, government and industry. The union representatives listened and, in their June, 1919, convention, voted to give blacks full membership in the union.

World War I ended on November 11, 1918, at 11 A.M.

Black troops did not have to wait long before they were returned home. Higher-ups in the U. S. military hierarchy had never liked the fraternization between the French and the black soldiers. An order had even gone out telling French officers not to socialize with black officers attached to their commands. With the fighting over, American officials gave top priority to the return of black soldiers.

Colonel William Hayward, commander of the 369th, had once paraded his new command (then the Fifteenth New York) through Harlem in a recruitment drive.

Training in France, black soldiers drill in setting up machine guns.

His troops were derided for their lack of military skills. Later, he was denied a request to be made a part of the famed "Rainbow Division" in New York City. It is said that he was told that black was not one of the colors of the rainbow. Later, his men were left out of the Twenty-seventh Division farewell parade.

Colonel Hayward promised his men that some day they would parade the streets of New York and when the war ended, he was able to keep that promise. The regiment which had left New York as a rather rag-tag group of embryo soldiers had been welded into a proud, precise marching organization that could honorably carry the ribbons of the Croix de Guerre on its colors. The regiment boasted the best band in the armed forces and had been honored not only for its performances on the battlefields of France but for the deportment of its men. The band, under the direction of the great jazz musician and band leader First Lieuten-

Black troops take instruction from French officers. Many black troops were brigaded with the French.

In a trench at the front, black troops prepare to defend their sector.

ant James Reese Europe, assisted by drum major Sergeant Noble Sissle, played before military and civilian leaders in town after town throughout France. A group of some ninety handpicked musicians, the 369th Infantry Band, was known as the band which brought jazz to France.

The 369th came home with honor, and on February 17, 1919, New York City gave the regiment its day of glory. The regiment paraded up Fifth Avenue where, less than two years earlier, the NAACP had staged a silent parade of men, women, and children in protest against the East St. Louis riot. There had been almost no spectators at the protest parade but those watching the 369th were conservatively estimated at 250,000. The governor, the mayor, aldermen, and other state and local officials crowded the review stand and thousands of women and children waved small flags as the regiment marched up Fifth Avenue. When the group reached Harlem, Colonel Hayward ordered his men to march with a normal interval between men and lines. He felt that in Lenox Avenue the men should parade so that each man could be seen by his friends and neighbors. They were seen —and as wives, mothers, and sweethearts spied their men they rushed to join them. By the end of the parade the report is that about every fourth marcher had from one to three women clinging to his arms.

Similar parades were repeated as other black units returned to their home towns.

A symbol of the heroism of the black soldiers was Sergeant Henry Johnson. In the parade of the 369th, the injured Johnson rode standing in a car carrying a bouquet of flowers. Johnson and Private Needham Roberts were probably the most acclaimed black heroes of World War I. Some time after 2 A.M. on the morning of May 14, 1918, the then Private Johnson and Private Roberts were part of a five-man force manning Observation Post 29 in the Montplaisir sector held by the First Battalion of the 369th. Germans had been filtering through the lines and sniping from the rear. Johnson and Roberts were on guard while the corporal and two other privates were off duty in the dugout of the post. Roberts heard a slight sound and got Johnson from the west side of the bunker. They listened and again they heard a noise like barbed wire being clipped. Both men shouted a warning to the corporal of the guard and fired an illuminating rocket. The Germans retaliated by throwing hand grenades into the post and both Roberts and Johnson were injured. The explosion of the grenades penned in the other members of the tiny garrison. Roberts propped himself up against the door of the dugout and, though gravely wounded, kept throwing grenades into the darkness. Johnson was on his feet with his rifle when the Germans rushed the enclosure. Johnson quickly fired the three shots from his Labelle rifle, killing at least one man. He then swung his rifle at the head of a German, felling him to the ground. Turning, he saw two Germans

Soldiers from the 370th Infantry Regiment return to Chicago on a troop train. The 372nd Infantry Regiment (below) paraded in Boston.

Hero Sergeant Henry Johnson stood in a car in the 369th's parade up Fifth Avenue. He and Needham Roberts (inset) were the first American blacks to win the Croix de Guerre.

trying to carry Roberts away as a prisoner. Johnson leaped forward with his bolo knife and stabbed one of them to death. The German he had clubbed to the ground recovered and opened fire. Johnson was hit again and dropped to all fours as the man came at him. As soon as the German got within reach, Johnson leaped up and disemboweled him with the bolo knife. The German patrol panicked, snatched up their dead and wounded and fled. As they left, Johnson continued to hurl grenades at them.

When reinforcements finally arrived, the Germans had disappeared, leaving behind them some forty grenades, seven long-arm wire clippers, three automatics and three caps. The patrol of some twenty-four men had been routed by two wounded black privates.

Henry Johnson could have been discharged early but he wanted to stay with the 369th to the end. Though crippled, he was promoted to sergeant and remained for the parade of glory. Roberts, from Trenton, New Jersey, did not return to the regiment. Ten days after the parade, Sergeant Johnson asked for his discharge from the army. The hero of the 369th went back to his job as a porter at an Albany, New York, railroad station.

Many black soldiers returned to cotton chopping and portering and waiting on tables. But the war had done something to emancipate many black men. They had gone abroad to fight for democracy, they had seen life in a nation relatively free from black-white racism, they had seen the cities of the North, and they had learned skills.

The change affected not only soldiers. Black civilians had learned that the world extended beyond their formerly narrow horizons and they began to aspire to travel far, not only physically but psychologically. Black people were ready for the next step forward. It was to be a trying and bloody one.

Watching the 369th parade, a wounded black soldier gave mute testimony of the sacrifices made by black men.

5

Renaissance

In July, 1918, in what he later called "one of my periods of exhaltation," editor W. E. B. Du Bois published his famed editorial, "Close Ranks." In the pages of *The Crisis*, official voice of the NAACP, he said, in part, "That which the German power represents today spells death to the aspirations of Negroes and all darker races for equality, freedom and democracy. Let us not hesitate. Let us, while this war lasts, forget our special grievances and close our ranks shoulder to shoulder with our own white fellow citizens and the allied nations that are fighting for democracy. We make no ordinary sacrifice, but we make it gladly and willingly with our eyes lifted to the hills."

The editorial came at a time when black soldiers were proving their valor overseas and President Wilson had finally spoken out against lynching. Still, it provoked a great deal of criticism from other blacks, which Du Bois felt that he had to answer.

> First [he said, in the August *Crisis*], this is Our Country—we have worked for it, we have suffered for it, we have fought for it; we have made its music, we have tinged its ideals, its poetry, its religion, its dreams; we have reached in this land our highest modern development and nothing, humanly speaking, can prevent us from eventually reaching here the full stature of our manhood. Our country is at war. The war is critical, dangerous and world-wide. If this is our country, then this is our war. We must fight it with every ounce of blood and treasure . . . . But what of our wrongs, cry a million voices with strained faces and bitter eyes. Our wrongs are still wrong. War does not excuse disfranchisement, "Jim Crow" cars and social injustices, but it does make our first duty clear. It does say deep to the heart of every Negro American—we will not bargain with our loyalty. We will not profiteer with our country's blood. . . .

Judging from the loyalty displayed by black Americans during the war, Du Bois seems to have spoken for the masses. Less

KEEP
RIGHT

than a year later, he seems to have spoken for the black soldiers then being discharged from the services when he wrote:

> We return from the slavery of uniform which the world's madness demanded us don to the freedom of civil garb. We stand again to look America squarely in the face and call a spade a spade. We sing: This country of ours, despite all its better souls have done and dreamed, is yet a shameful land.

The Harlem of the 1920s with its wide streets and big buildings attracted blacks. Here children are leaving Public School 89 at 135th Street and Lenox Avenue.

> It lynches . . . it disfranchises its own citizens . . . it encourages ignorances . . . it insults us. . . .
>
> We return. We return from fighting. We return fighting. Make way for Democracy! We saved it in France, and by the Great Jehovah, we will save it in the U.S.A., or know the reason why.

The nearly four hundred thousand black soldiers who were as rapidly as possible returned to civilian life were soon searching for "the reason why."

In the year 1919, democracy seemed a hollow mockery to most black people. During the war, the Ku Klux Klan had grown in power and by 1919 it was active against blacks not only throughout the South, but in the North and Midwest.

From June through December, 1919, seventy-six blacks were lynched and there

were twenty-five race riots. Among those lynched were ten black soldiers, some of them still wearing their uniforms. Three soldiers were killed in Georgia and three more in Mississippi, two were lynched in Arkansas and mobs killed one in Florida and one in Alabama. In Omaha, Nebraska, a mob not only lynched and burned a black man, but hanged the white mayor who tried to prevent the lynching, and burned down the courthouse. The ferocity of the whites rivaled the atrocities of which the Germans had been accused during World War I. They burned black men alive and then fought over scraps of clothing or pieces of the body as souvenirs. Men, women, and even unborn children were the victims of lynch mobs.

The NAACP had made lynching and segregation its main targets and it had to take to the courts many times just to secure its right to operate as a civil rights organization. In 1919, the state of Texas attempted to stop the NAACP from operating by claiming that it was not chartered to do business in Texas. John Shillady, a white man who was national secretary of the organization, went to Texas to defend the NAACP as a civic and educational body in August, 1919. A white mob beat him unconscious on the streets in Austin. He resigned the next year and was succeeded by poet and writer James Weldon Johnson, an NAACP field secretary who named the summer of 1919 "The Red Summer." And a "red" summer it was.

Race riots occurred in the South, East, West, and Midwest, in cities as large as Chicago and Washington, D.C., and as small as Longview, Texas, and Elaine, Arkansas.

The riot in the nation's capital started on July 19, when gangs of white soldiers, sailors, and marines, egged on by rumormongers who claimed that black men had been assaulting white women, invaded black neighborhoods, beating up black men—even pursuing some of them into their homes. The attacks persisted for a second day and it is said that three black men were killed. On the third day, white gangs attempted to invade and burn black neighborhoods but found to their surprise that black men had secured guns and were

Harlem housewives shopped at open vegetable stands at 135th Street and Fifth Avenue (left). Jazz Age couple were captured by famed black photographer James Van Derzee.

The Garvey movement featured a paramilitary organization and elaborate uniforms. Here a group drills on a Harlem street during a parade.

fighting back. It is estimated that several whites were killed and many others injured before the city called out the U.S. Provost Guard to restore order.

That same month in Longview, Texas, a group of white men went into a black neighborhood in search of a Negro who was supposed to have sent reports of a lynching to the *Chicago Defender*. Blacks fired on the invaders, hitting several of them. The next day, whites turned out in force, burning several houses in the black neighborhood, beating up several leading citizens and running others out of town.

The Longview and Washington riots brought a new dimension to racial strife in America. Where in the past whites had been allowed to ravage as they pleased, blacks were now fighting back. It remained for the "riot" in Chicago to carry the movement to its logical conclusion—a pitched battle between blacks and whites that rivaled some of the skirmishes of World War I.

Racial tension had built up in the city because of the tremendous migration of blacks from the South. The ghetto's seams were straining as some one hundred thousand blacks sought living space. As blacks tried to spread into white neighborhoods, the whites responded with threats and bombings. Invisible lines were drawn and to cross them invited retaliation. The "invisible lines" stretched even to the beaches of Lake Michigan where blacks and whites swam in segregated water. The

Photographer Van Derzee (2nd from l. below) preserved images of his family and relatives on film in the early 1920s.

The NAACP waged a vigorous fight against lynching. On November 23, 1922, this advertisement appeared in the *New York Times*, *Atlanta Constitution* and other newspapers in support of the Dyer antilynching bill.

THE SHAME OF AMERICA

Do you know that the United States is the Only Land on Earth where human beings are BURNED AT THE STAKE?

In Four Years 1918-1921, Twenty-Eight People were publicly
BURNED BY AMERICAN MOBS

3436 People Lynched, 1889-1921

For What Crimes Have Mobs Nullified Government and Inflicted the Death Penalty?

The Alleged Crimes	The Victims	Why Some Mob Victims Died
Murder	1288	Not turning out of road for white boy in auto
Rape	571	Being a relative of a person who was lynched
Crimes against the Person	615	Jumping a labor contract
Crimes against Property	333	Being a member of the Non-Partisan League
Miscellaneous Crimes	453	"Talking back" to a white man
Absence of Crime	176	"Insulting" white man
	3436	

Is Rape the "Cause" of Lynching?

Of 3,436 people murdered by mobs in our country, only 571, or less than 17 per cent, were even accused of the crime of rape.

83 WOMEN HAVE BEEN LYNCHED IN THE UNITED STATES

Do lynchers maintain that they were lynched for "the usual crime"?

AND THE LYNCHERS GO UNPUNISHED

THE REMEDY

The Dyer Anti-Lynching Bill Is Now Before the United States Senate

The Dyer Anti-Lynching Bill was passed on January 26, 1922, by a vote of 230 to 119 in the House of Representatives.

The Dyer Anti-Lynching Bill Provides:

That culpable State officers and mobbists shall be tried in Federal Courts on failure of State courts to act, and that a county in which a lynching occurs shall be fined $10,000, recoverable in a Federal Court.

The Principal Question Raised Against the Bill is upon the Ground of Constitutionality.

The Constitutionality of the Dyer Bill Has Been Affirmed by:

The Judiciary Committee of the House of Representatives
The Judiciary Committee of the Senate
The United States Attorney General, legal adviser of Congress
Judge Guy D. Goff, of the Department of Justice

The Senate has been petitioned to pass the Dyer Bill by

29 Lawyers and Jurists including two former Attorneys General of the United States
19 State Supreme Court Justices
24 State Governors
3 Archbishops, 85 bishops and prominent churchmen
39 Mayors of large cities, north and south

The American Bar Association at its meeting in San Francisco, August 9, 1922, adopted a resolution asking for further legislation by Congress to punish and prevent lynching and mob violence.

Fifteen State Conventions of 1922 (3 of them Democratic) have inserted in their party platforms a demand for national action to stamp out lynchings.

The Dyer Anti-Lynching Bill is not intended to protect the guilty, but to assure to every person accused of crime trial by due process of law.

THE DYER ANTI-LYNCHING BILL IS NOW BEFORE THE SENATE
TELEGRAPH YOUR SENATORS TODAY YOU WANT IT ENACTED

If you want to help the organization which has brought to light the facts about lynching, the organization which is fighting for 100 per cent Americanism, not for some of the people some of the time, but for all of the people, white or black, all of the time

Send your check to J. E. SPINGARN, Treasurer of the

NATIONAL ASSOCIATION FOR THE ADVANCEMENT OF COLORED PEOPLE

70 FIFTH AVENUE, NEW YORK CITY

THIS ADVERTISEMENT IS PAID FOR IN PART BY THE ANTI-LYNCHING CRUSADERS

A. Philip Randolph was a young militant who took an anti-establishment stand and won victories, especially for labor.

battle is said to have started when seventeen-year-old Eugene Williams floated or swam from "black" to "white" water. Whites stoned him, and he drowned. Although investigators said his body showed no signs of having been hit by stones, the story was out and blacks on the beach even pointed out the white man who was supposed to have hit him. When police refused to arrest the man, the blacks attacked the police and the battle was joined. Both whites and blacks were injured in the battle on the beach and rumors spread throughout the city. The incident took place on Sunday. On Monday morning, blacks going to work in white neighborhoods were attacked. Blacks in turn attacked whites in black neighborhoods. The battle spread and by Wednesday the governor had called out the National Guard. Sniping, burning, looting, and beatings were taking place over such a widespread area that it was thirteen days before peace was finally restored. The casualties were appalling. Twenty-three blacks and fifteen whites lay dead. Some 537 persons, including 178 whites, had been wounded and more than 1,000 families (mostly black) were homeless.

The extent of the Chicago riot shocked both white and black leaders but the wave continued as major outbreaks occurred over a wide area.

Many of the Red Summer riots grew out of the fact that a new militancy had developed not only among national leaders but among the masses in towns throughout the nation. The militancy of the period was probably best exemplified in the body of the NAACP.

By 1920, the NAACP was led primarily by black men in the field, although it was still controlled by an interracial board of directors and fought for integration. A good example of the work it was doing can be drawn from the Elaine, Arkansas, riot and its aftermath. Black farmers wanted to organize a union to protest against the low prices being paid for cotton by the white buyers. They met in October and the meeting was broken up by a deputy sheriff and a posse. In the resulting fracas, the deputy was killed.

Marcus Garvey had a charisma that swayed millions.

Whites immediately retaliated. Reports of the number of blacks killed vary widely. More than one hundred were wounded. After the shooting had died down, seventy-nine blacks were brought to trial and twelve of them were sentenced to death for murder and insurrection. The rest were given long prison sentences.

The NAACP investigated the riot and took on the defense of the accused. Raising $50,000 as a defense fund, the NAACP won reversal of the convictions of the twelve men sentenced to death, and by 1925 the last of the imprisoned sixty-seven had been freed.

The NAACP was famous not only for its legal work but for its crusading publication, *The Crisis*. Founded in 1910, *The Crisis* had sold some four-and-one-half million copies by 1920. Its circulation reached one-hundred thousand a month in 1919 and it grossed over $70,000 in 1920. *The Crisis* was not only the voice of the NAACP but a literary magazine, an outlet for black poets and essayists and a platform for Du Bois, one of the most out-

standing minds—white or black—of the twentieth century.

The goal of the NAACP was to secure full citizenship rights for black Americans, and the leaders learned early that the path toward full equality for blacks was an obstacle course, with one of the biggest barriers being the widespread use of lynching to intimidate Negroes.

The outlawing of lynching was therefore given top priority on the NAACP's program. Because lynching was such a heinous crime, it was not difficult to rally support for a federal antilynching bill among liberal and influential whites in the North. But passage of such a bill in Congress was difficult. It was made even more difficult because Southern politicians traded their support of pet Northern bills for support or abstentions or just being absent when antilynch legislation came before the House or Senate. As early as 1919, the NAACP got Republican L. C. Dyer of Missouri to introduce an antilynching bill in the House. The bill, over the vigorous objections of Southern representatives, was passed in the House, but despite petitions by hundreds of liberal whites (including twenty-four governors), it was never brought to vote in the Senate because of a Southern filibuster. Other antilynching bills suffered a similar fate.

Stymied on the legal front, the NAACP

Garvey (opposite page) was resplendent in uniform and plumes as he reviewed a parade. Handcuffed (below), he entered the federal penitentiary in Atlanta to begin a five-year term for fraudulent use of the mails.

took its antilynching crusade to the streets. It published a book, *Thirty Years of Lynching In The United States, 1889–1918,* which detailed in all their horror the thousands of lynchings perpetrated during that time. Walter White, who was later to have a distinguished career as national secretary to the NAACP, was hired as an investigator of crimes against black people. The NAACP published reports on all lynchings and in 1929, White published *Rope and Faggot, A Biography Of Judge Lynch.*

The NAACP also sought voting rights for black citizens in the South, filing suits to open up primaries in one-party states where election in the Democratic primary was tantamount to election to office.

The NAACP was strong nationally, not only because it had strong national leadership backed by the wealth and support of white liberals such as Joel Spingarn, but because it established chapters in almost every state and major city in the country. By 1919 there were three hundred branches of the NAACP: 122 in the North with 38,420 members; 155 in the South with 42,588 members, and 33 in the West with 7,440 members. In most cities, the NAACP leader was one of the most influential black men in town. Sociologist E. Franklin Frazier has commented on the fact that although the leadership of the NAACP was drawn from black intellectuals and their friends among white intellectual liberals, it still won the support of the masses during the 1920s and 1930s. During that period the organization boasted such names as Du Bois, James Weldon Johnson, Walter White, Charles H. Houston, Thurgood Marshall, William Hastie, and Roy Wilkins.

A second interracial organization aimed at easing discrimination and improving relationships between whites and blacks in the South was organized in 1919. Called the Commission on Interracial Cooperation, it was organized by William W. Alexander with offices in Atlanta, Georgia and chapters in the various states of the South. The commission attempted to bring about better racial understanding through meetings and seminars on a state or community level.

At the end of World War I, the NAACP, perturbed over reports of the mistreatment of black soldiers abroad, decided to send W. E. B. Du Bois to France to investigate. He was also asked to collect and perfect information on the participation of black soldiers abroad.

The appointment came at an opportune time, for Du Bois and a number of other black Americans had been discussing the advisability and necessity of having the American Negro and black people of the world represented at the Peace Congress in France. Du Bois and others were interested not only because of the participation of black Americans in the war but because the Peace Conference would have direct bearing on what was to happen to the French, Belgian, British, Portuguese, and German colonies in Africa.

Since the Peace Congress at Versailles was concerned with nations still legally at war, it was evident to Du Bois that he would not be permitted to appear before the congress. He then determined to call a Pan-African Congress in Paris.

The 1920s saw the introduction of works by Jean Toomer (r.) whose book *Cane* appeared in 1923 and Countee Cullen, whose first collection of poems, *Color*, was published in 1925.

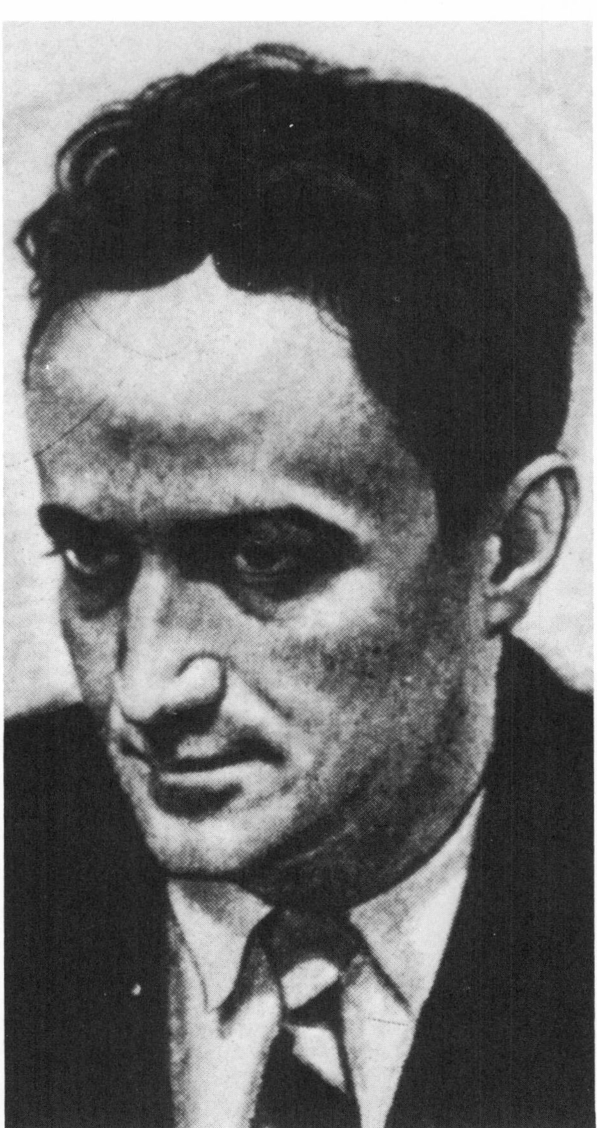

Du Bois's attempt to hold a Pan-African Congress would have failed miserably if it were not for the fact that black Africa had the right to send a black member from Senegal to the French Parliament. As high commissioner from Senegal during World War I, Blaise Daigne was responsible for 180,000 black soldiers coming from Africa to face the German élite troops in Flanders Field. The French respected Daigne and when he interceded with Clemenceau, Du Bois, over the protest of the American government, was given permission to hold a Pan-African Congress in February, 1919, at the Grand Hotel in Paris.

Despite the opposition of the English and the Americans, the congress attracted fifty-seven delegates, including sixteen American Negroes, twenty West Indians and twelve Africans. The French, Belgians, and Portuguese sent official representatives, but the British refused their

Claude McKay was known as a poet in his native Jamaica before moving to New York.

delegates passports and the Americans withheld official recognition.

Du Bois admitted that this first congress had limited results but the very fact that it was held was significant. His experiences with this congress were the first in a line of events which revealed to Du Bois what he believed to be the crux of the problems of his time, "The widespread efforts of white Europe to use the labor and material of the colored world for its own wealth and power."

As the NAACP emissary, Du Bois did succeed admirably in his investigation of the treatment of black troops abroad. He not only listened to black soldiers, but he also talked to and collected documents from the French proving that American officers had demanded that the French behave insultingly to Negroes. When his reports were published in *The Crisis*, the magazine sold more than one hundred thousand copies.

Alain Locke was essayist, critic, and philosopher of the Harlem Renaissance.

The limited success of the first, hurriedly planned Pan-African Congress gave Du Bois and his friends enough encouragement to continue to try to increase contacts of "Negroes of different origins and nationality."

With this in mind, Du Bois planned a second Pan-African Congress which, between August 29 and September 6, in 1921, sat successively in London, Brussels, and Paris. Du Bois ran into a good deal of opposition during the planning of his second congress. He says he found that the board of directors of the NAACP was not particularly interested and that the liberalism of American whites did not extend to Africa and to colored peoples outside the United States. There was also opposition from some American blacks. But Du Bois and his friends persevered and the second Pan-African Congress was much more successful than the first. There were 113 accredited delegates from twenty-six different groups in attendance. The U.S.

James Weldon Johnson combined brilliant careers as writer and executive secretary of the NAACP.

delegation consisted of thirty-five delegates and there were thirty-nine from the African continent. The rest came from the West Indies and Europe. The congress was addressed by British, French, Spanish, and Belgian dignitaries and received press coverage in all the leading papers of Europe. Belgians in Brussels heatedly debated the right of the congress to discuss the relation of European countries to their colonies in Africa. The congress drew up petitions and suggestions which Du Bois and others presented to the League of Nations and the International Labor Office.

A third Pan-African Congress was held in 1923, meeting in London, Paris, and Lisbon. Following this congress, Du Bois made his first visit to Africa. In Sierra Leone he met with members of the Congress of West Africa, an organization which he described as being similar to the NAACP.

The fourth Pan-African Congress was held in New York City in 1927. Du Bois

Langston Hughes was one of the most sophisticated and prolific writers of the Renaissance.

Arna Bontemps started writing in California, but later became a part of the Harlem Renaissance.

and his friends admitted that it was held, "just to keep the idea alive."

Another venture in Pan-Africanism was led by a charismatic Jamaican who burst almost full bloom on the black American scene in 1916. The man was Marcus Garvey, who in a few years was to become the most widely known black man in the world.

Marcus Moziah Garvey was born on the northern coast of Jamaica in a little town called St. Ann's on August 17, 1887. He was the youngest of eleven children but only Marcus and a sister, Indiana, lived to maturity. Garvey's parents were not poverty stricken when he was a child, his father being a stonemason and his mother sometimes adding to the family income by selling cakes and pastries. Little is known of his early schooling. Garvey's formal education probably ended when he reached fourteen and was apprenticed to learn the printing trade. At seventeen, he left St. Ann's to work at his trade with an uncle in Kingston, the capital of Jamaica. An ambitious young man, Marcus advanced rapidly as a printer and

Sterling Brown wrote during the 1920s and was adviser to the Federal Writers' Project during the Depression.

also as an orator by constantly participating in the street debates which were a popular pastime in Kingston. At twenty he was a master printer and a foreman at one of the largest printing firms in Jamaica. When the Printers Union struck in 1907, Garvey went out on strike with the workers despite the fact that he was a foreman. He was chosen to lead the strike but his men finally capitulated after the union treasurer absconded with the funds and the printers began bringing in linotype machines. Most of the strikers were rehired but Garvey, the only foreman who had joined the strike, was blacklisted. This experience made him contemptuous of labor unions and later in New York he remained skeptical of the value of the labor movement.

Garvey next went to work at the government printing house. His experience with the union had made him realize that the black man needed some kind of organization to help him and he made several attempts to start one. He also realized the need for communication and started to publish a periodical called *Garvey's Watchman* and later another called *Our Own*. A very dark man of unmixed stock, Garvey found that in Jamaica the whites

Wallace Thurman wrote fiction *(The Blacker The Berry*, 1929) during the late Renaissance.

Sociologist Charles Johnson edited *Opportunity Magazine* featuring Renaissance writers.

and the mulattoes had the best jobs, the most money, and the most power. He resented this and left Jamaica for Costa Rica, where he hoped to earn enough money to return and start an organization to help Jamaican blacks. For the next few years Garvey traveled throughout Central and South America and finally, in 1912, he settled briefly in London. Here he met a half-Negro, half-Egyptian author, Duse Mohammed Ali, who published a monthly magazine, the *Africa Times and Orient Review*. From this man and the many African students and workers he met, Garvey learned a lot about Africa. It was here also that he first read Booker T. Washington's *Up From Slavery* and he said, ". . . . then my doom—if I may so call it—of being a race leader dawned on me . . . I asked, 'Where is the black man's government? Where is his king and his kingdom? Where is his President, his country, and his ambassador, his army, his navy, his men of big affairs? I could not find them, and then I declared, I will help to make them.' "

Hurrying home to Jamaica in the summer of 1914, Garvey had his mind set on the possibility of "uniting all the Negro peoples of the world into one great body to establish a country and Government absolutely their own."

Within a month after his return to Kingston, Garvey had gathered together some of his old friends and had organized the Universal Negro Improvement and Conservation Association and African Communities League. The manifesto of the new organization called for "all people of Negro or African parentage" to join in a great crusade to rehabilitate the race. The Universal Negro Improvement Association, as it came to be known, soon had its own constitution, motto, and staff of officers. Garvey was named president and traveling commissioner. The associate secretary was a young woman named Amy Ashwood. She was later to become the first Mrs. Marcus Garvey.

The young organization received unexpected support from whites, including the mayor of Kingston, a Roman Catholic bishop, and the governor of the island when it first came out for the establishment of educational and industrial colleges for blacks patterned after Booker T. Washington's Tuskegee Institute. But most blacks were indifferent to the U.N.I.A. Garvey decided to go to the United States to visit Booker T. Washington and to find out how he could raise money for his schools in Jamaica, but before he could make the trip, Washington died.

The next year, Garvey decided that he would go to the United States even though his idol was no longer alive, and on March 23, 1916, Marcus Garvey arrived in Har-

Carter G. Woodson founded the Association for the Study of Negro Life and History in 1916.

lem. At first his work in the United States was not very productive. The first year he visited some thirty-eight states and talked to black leaders, but it wasn't until June 12, 1917, that he had a chance to address a large gathering in Harlem. At a mass meeting held at the Bethel African Methodist Episcopal Church for the purpose of organizing the Liberty League, Garvey was introduced to the audience and spoke eloquently about the new organization.

Garvey had planned to start a New York division of the UNIA and then return to Jamaica. His first attempts to organize in New York met with little success.

When, in 1917, a UNIA branch of several hundred members was finally organized in New York, Garvey discovered that some of the members were trying to turn it into a political club. Intra-group rivalry broke up that group and Garvey had to start again. This time the Harlem

Chemist George Washington Carver discovered new uses for agricultural products such as the peanut. From 1896 until his death he worked at the Tuskegee Institute.

branch grew to some fifteen hundred members before the politicians again tried to take over the group. Leaders loyal to Garvey asked him to assume personal leadership and he accepted. Elected president-general of the Harlem Branch although still president of the parent group, Garvey moved quickly to reorganize the branch as a membership corporation under New York law in order to protect its name. Under its New York charter, the UNIA promised to "promote and practice the principles of benevolence" and described its purpose as "the protection and social intercourse of its members."

Garvey boasted that in the three weeks after he assumed leadership, the New York branch took in two thousand new members. It was the beginning of one of the largest mass movements among black people.

Any thoughts Garvey may have harbored of returning to Jamaica were soon dispelled. Black people were not really interested in industrial schools in Jamaica, they were interested in Garvey's talk of the greatness of the black man, the greatness of Africa, and the fight of the proud black man to reclaim Africa from European colonial control. Faced daily with segregation and discrimination, plagued with feelings of inferiority, the last hired and the first fired, hearing daily tales of lynchings, black Americans welcomed this black spellbinder who told them how great they were and how, through his organization, they could become even greater. He didn't promise "pie in the sky" as the ministers did; he promised economic betterment, a more noble status, and the dignity of being a man.

The Western world became Garvey's hunting ground. He sought followers throughout the United States, traveling to every state of the Union to start new chap-

ters of the UNIA. He reached out to blacks in the West Indies, Central and South America and initiated chapters there. His fame spread to Europe and Africa.

In January, 1918, Garvey established the *Negro World*, a weekly newspaper devoted "solely to the interests of the Negro Race." A well-edited, well-written "house organ" for the UNIA, the *Negro World* was first distributed in New York City but it soon had subscribers all over the United States. Estimates of its circulation run as high as two hundred thousand weekly but it is more likely that it sold somewhere around fifty thousand as it claimed in its August 2, 1920, issue, though its circulation could well have been higher in the peak Garvey years from 1920 to 1922.

No one will ever know exactly how many members the UNIA eventually attracted. Garvey claimed two million members in 1919 in just thirty branches which would have meant an average of sixty-six thousand members per branch. In 1923 he claimed eleven million members. His opponents, and he had many of them, especially among the black American intellectuals, usually estimated his membership at less than one hundred thousand but this would still have been the largest black organization in the world.

Recognizing the power of money, Garvey felt that capitalism could be used to help the black man. In keeping with his grandiose style, Garvey decided he would start a black-owned steamship line. At UNIA meetings, money was collected to buy ships for this company. This seemingly innocent practice marked the beginning of the end for Marcus Garvey. When Edwin P. Kilrod, assistant district attorney of New York City, heard that Garvey was collecting money as investments in the Black Star Line, he warned Garvey not to attempt to sell stock unless the company was legally organized and registered. Garvey then formally incorporated The Black Star Line as a Delaware corporation. The company was incorporated at $500,000 with one hundred thousand shares of stock authorized at five dollars a share. Garvey and four others had bought forty shares each, putting $1,000 in the firm's treasury.

Booker T. Washington had taught that black men should own their own businesses to become independent of whites and when it was announced that here was a business in which any black man (sales were restricted to blacks) could own a share for just five dollars, the black masses were duly impressed.

Skeptics in New York felt that Garvey was just out to fleece the masses and others

Dr. Ernest Everett Just was a biologist and Howard University professor noted for his work on chromosome structure in animals. He was awarded the first Spingarn Medal in 1915.

The Lafayette Theater on 7th Avenue near 131st Street in 1927. Legitimate plays as well as musical revues were presented here.

felt that while he might be sincere, he was venturing into a field of which he and his fellow workers had little or no experience and that they were bound to fail.

Garvey confounded his critics. Before the end of the year 1919, the Black Star Line had its first ship, the *Yarmouth*, flying the red, black, and green flag adopted by the line, ready for a voyage to the West Indies.

The Black Star Line bought two other vessels, an excursion boat and a steam yacht, neither of which was commercially successful.

In its first year of business, the Black Star Line took in $610,860 through the sale of stock and subscriptions. The company had spent $617,255.65. Unfortunately, the money had not been spent wisely. Within two years, Garvey was arrested for using the mails to defraud in the sale of Black Star Line stock and for selling passages to Africa on a mythical vessel. He was also accused of selling memberships in false and fraudulent organizations. The Black Star Line was bankrupt and the UNIA had been dealt a damaging blow.

The years 1920 and 1921 were the heyday of Garvey's organization. His black nationalism had reached to even the smallest town and his annual conventions in New York City were the biggest black events in the nation's history. The colorful uniforms of the officials, the precision of the marching bands, the pomp and ceremony of formal gatherings made the conventions a spectators' delight. In 1920,

VAUDEVILLE
LAFAYETTE
THEATRE
THE FINEST
COLORED MUSICAL REVUES

Josephine Baker played in Sissle and Blake's *Chocolate Dandies* in 1924, went to Paris in 1925, and later starred at the Folies Bergeres.

more than twenty-five thousand blacks were in Madison Square Garden to hear Garvey speak. "We are the descendants of a suffering people," he told the crowd, "we are the descendants of a people determined to suffer no longer. We shall now organize the four hundred million Negroes of the world into a vast organization to plant the banner of freedom on the great continent of Africa."

The opponents of Garvey were men like Du Bois, James Weldon Johnson, George Schuyler, A. Philip Randolph, and others who believed that he was a charlatan leading the masses astray. Garvey challenged organizations like the NAACP and the Urban League which preached and practiced an interracial philosophy. There were rumors that the Klan lent support to Garvey.

In addition to his steamship line, Garvey chartered the Negro Factories Corporation capitalized at one million dollars and sold shares for five dollars each. This company was to start factories for black people all over the world. The firm did start a grocery chain, a restaurant, a millinery store, a publishing company, and several other small businesses. It was also supposed to make loans to blacks going into business and to give them counseling. Garvey's principal organization, the Universal Negro Improvement Association, was also set up as a fraternal business organization similar to an insurance company. Members were supposed to pay monthly dues and were to be paid sickness and death benefits from the national treasury.

On June 21, 1923, Marcus Garvey, president general of UNIA and provisional president of Africa, was found guilty of using the mails to defraud. He was sentenced to five years in prison and fined one thousand dollars and costs. He served as

A concert singer, Roland Hayes was awarded the Spingarn Medal in 1924.

his own lawyer and said later that most of his troubles came from black opponents. Garvey appealed his case, this time using white lawyers, up to the U. S. Circuit Court of Appeals, but again he lost and on February 8, 1925, he entered the federal penitentiary at Atlanta.

Prison walls did not still the voice of Marcus Garvey. He wrote letters regularly from prison and in December, 1925, Amy Jacques Garvey (his second wife), published a book of his speeches and writings. His followers continued to celebrate his birthday, August 17, as a holiday. Many of the UNIA chapters were still active and even some of his former enemies began to feel that he had not been treated fairly. Black America began a campaign for his release and finally President Calvin Coolidge commuted his sentence. Because he was an alien and had been convicted of a felony, Garvey was deported. Early in December, 1927, he was taken from the prison to New Orleans and put on a ship bound for Jamaica. Early in August, 1929, he held the Sixth International Convention of the Negro Peoples of the World in

Florence Mills starred in *Shuffle Along* in 1922. Some 150,000 watched her funeral procession in 1927.

Kingston, Jamaica, and his uniformed African Legion, Black Cross Nurses and the Universal Motor Corps paraded as they had in Harlem. The mayor of Kingston was in Edelweis Park to welcome Garvey and to congratulate him on the size of the convention. The conference was a success and on the final night some ten thousand people crammed Edelweis Park to watch the UNIA recreate what Garvey called "the court life of ancient Africa."

From here on, Garvey's road was all downhill. He served three months in jail on a contempt of court sentence in Jamaica. He wanted the headquarters of his organization in Jamaica, but his lieutenants believed that they should remain in New York. Eventually the group split and there were two UNIAs. Garvey had trouble within the ranks of his Jamaican division and in 1935 he moved his headquarters to London. There he died—never having set foot in Africa, the continent he believed to be the salvation of the black man.

While Marcus Garvey dominated the early 1920s, he was by no means the only strong leader to challenge white America. Post-war America was in a ferment and black America was going through changes even more dramatic and drastic than those faced by the whites.

At the war's end, some four million

Charles Gilpin managed the Lafayette Theater Company in Harlem, and played in *Abraham Lincoln* on Broadway in 1919.

men, four hundred thousand of them black, returned to the job market and jobs began to be hard to find, especially for blacks, even though the country as a whole was supposed to be booming. The stock market kept going up and up, but for black folk, the bubble had already burst long before the crash of 1929. They could not depend upon labor unions to protect them on their jobs, for most of the labor unions discriminated against blacks.

In New York a group of radicals organized The Friends of Negro Freedom in 1920 with plans to unionize migrant workers and cure numerous other racial ills, but it was largely ineffective and folded three years later. About the same time, two bright young men, Chandler Owen and A. Philip Randolph, tried to organize, with the help of white radicals, the National Association for the Promotion of Labor Unionism Among Negroes. This group failed after a futile attempt to organize black laundry workers.

Owen, a young law student at Columbia, and Randolph, a poor boy from Florida who had worked his way to New York to attend City College, met at a time when radicalism was all the rage among white intellectuals and college students.

Randolph and Owen set up a small employment bureau and training program for unskilled Negroes arriving from the

Paul Robeson played opposite Mary Blair in *All God's Chillun Got Wings* (below), and in *Emperor Jones* in 1925.

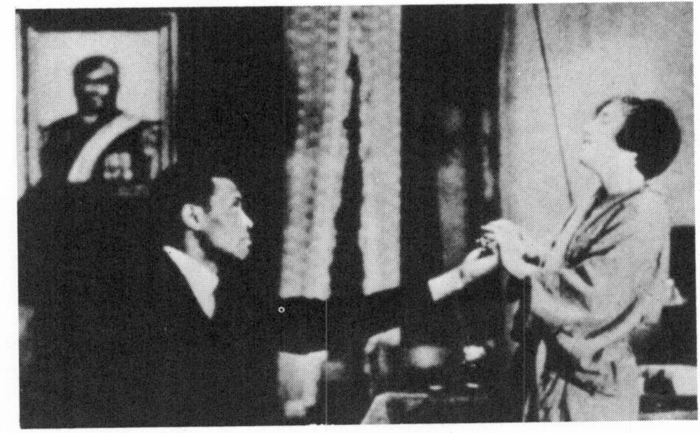

South. They called their business The Brotherhood and through it they were commissioned to publish a paper, *The Hotel Messenger*, for a new union of black head waiters. The two young men found out that the head waiters were cheating the men who worked under them. Owens and Randolph printed this news in the *Messenger*. The Brotherhood lost its client but retained the publication and *The Messenger* became one of the most outspoken papers in New York. The editors were harassed by the FBI and were even jailed for urging black men to refuse to be drafted into a Jim Crow Army in World War I.

Noble Sissle took a band to Paris in 1929 and teamed with Eubie Blake (r.) in writing words and music to such tunes as "Love Will Find A Way" and "I'm Just Wild About Harry."

The *Messenger* earned such a reputation for Randolph that when, in 1925, Ashley L. Totten was dismissed by the Pullman Company for trying to organize a union, he sought Randolph's aid. Totten knew that since 1909 every porter who became involved in organizing a union had been fired. He believed that it would be best to get an outsider to do the job and felt that Randolph was just that outsider. Meeting secretly first with six and later a select group of fifty porters, Randolph transacted all business himself. The Brotherhood of Sleeping Car Porters was organized and the members elected Randolph president. This marked the beginning of a twelve-year struggle for recognition of the union as the bargaining agent for the porters. During that time, some eight hundred porters were fired but they took other jobs and remained members of the union in order to keep it alive. The company, in desperation, reportedly offered a check of $10,000, a monumental sum at that time, to Randolph if he would withdraw. He refused and, in 1935, the black union won its fight.

The movement of black men from the

W.C. Handy started his first band in 1893, and played at the Columbian Exposition in Chicago. The musical giant composed "The St. Louis Blues." He was born in 1873, died in 1953.

South to the North was mainly for economic and social reasons. The jobs were in the North and in the North there was a certain freedom from fear of the lynch mob. But the mass movement North gave blacks a bonus that most had not thought of before. In the ghettos of New York, Chicago, Detroit, and Philadelphia, black people found themselves so segregated that eventually whole wards and congressional districts were filled with blacks.

As black politicians began to rise and black voters became more sophisticated, black office-holders increased. As an example, Republican Oscar DePriest was elected to the city council in Chicago in 1915. In 1928, DePriest was elected to the House of Representatives in Washington, D.C., the first black man since Reconstruction to sit in Congress.

From the very beginning, New York City was one of the most important cities in the United States. Settled first by the Dutch in 1613 when they built Fort Manhattan on the island which Peter Minuit later bought from the Indians for some twenty-four dollars' worth of baubles and beads, the colony was later taken by the British. The Dutch called it New Amsterdam and long before the British took over and renamed it New York, there were two other villages in the area—Brooklyn and Harlem. It wasn't too long before New York City had engulfed them all, but there is some sort of poetic justice in the fact that Harlem has always remained something special in what most people think of as the world's leading city.

For many years after black men moved into New York, Harlem was still the home of the landed and the wealthy whites. They raced their harness horses on its wide streets and their black servants lived in another part of town near Wall Street.

New York has long been Number One in almost everything in the United States. It has been a magnet, attracting from all over the nation the most talented people in business, the arts, and the professions, as well as hustlers. New York is "The Big Apple" and, once Harlem turned black, it was only natural that the teeming city within a city would become synonymous with the best for black America.

The migration of masses of blacks from the South naturally brought thousands of black migrants to the city. Most of these came up the eastern coast from Florida, Georgia, Alabama, Virginia, the Carolinas, and Maryland, a natural path of migration. But there was, in the early twentieth century, another black influx to the city by the Hudson. This was a select migration of talented and ambitious blacks not only from the South, but from the West and Midwest, from other sections of the North and even from the islands of the West Indies. When these migrants joined the indigenous black intelligentsia of the metropolis in the years immediately following World War I, they sparked one of the most exciting and unusual periods in black American history—the Harlem Renaissance.

The black writers, artists, singers, dancers, actors, and musicians who flocked to Harlem came there because out of Harlem had come *The Crisis* and *Opportunity* magazines which had given them a chance to publish their stories and poems. New York had the theaters, the dance halls, the cabarets, and the nightclubs. Jim Europe and Noble Sissle had won in-

Discovered by Ma Rainey, Bessie Smith (opposite page) started her blues singing career at thirteen. Mamie Smith (left) made the first blues record, "Crazy Blues," in 1920.

Jazz giant Joseph (King) Oliver started career in New Orleans. In 1923, his second cornetist was young Louis Armstrong (opposite page).

ternational fame with New York's 369th Regimental Band. The young man in Cleveland or Wichita or any of the hundreds of Springfields throughout the country believed that if he could get to New York he would make it.

A. Philip Randolph had come from Florida and made it as the militant editor of *The Messenger*. James Weldon Johnson had left Florida to make his name in New York, both as a writer and National Secretary of the NAACP. T. Thomas Fortune edited the militant *New York Age* and its fame spread far beyond the confines of the city. Militant blacks, including Claude McKay, the Jamaican who had already earned a name for himself as a poet, had sailed from the West Indies to New York City. McKay had been awarded the medal of the Institute of Arts and Sciences in his native Jamaica in 1911 for his book of poetry, *Song of Jamaica*. He had studied at Tuskegee and the University of Kansas before settling in New York.

The black novelists, artists, poets, and dramatists of the Harlem Renaissance were men and women with a sense of social consciousness. They felt keenly their experiences and the experiences of their black brothers through the "war for democracy" and "the Red Summer." Some had seen lynchings and all had read of them. They were black people who cre-

ated out of their black experience and many of their creations were directed toward other blacks.

But the white world discovered the Harlem Renaissance. White writers like Theodore Dreiser and Sinclair Lewis were writing serious novels that questioned the values of the system. There was a trend among whites to create works of art that pointed out the flaws of a capitalistic democratic society with the aim of persuading others to weed out these flaws. Many white writers saw that one of the greatest flaws in this democratic society was the undemocratic treatment of the black man.

Wealthy and sincere whites like Joel Spingarn, himself a writer, and others connected with the NAACP and Urban League associated socially with blacks of the Renaissance. Wealthy white dilettantes gave parties downtown and invited a select number of black literary guests—or they took their white friends with them for "an evening in Harlem"—sometimes to lavish parties given by A'Lelia Walker, heiress to the Madame Walker hair straightener fortune.

It was during this period that Eugene O'Neill wrote *The Emperor Jones* and *All God's Chillun Got Wings* and another white writer, Paul Green, won the Pulitzer Prize with the play *In Abraham's Bosom*, produced on Broadway with a predominantly black cast.

In some ways, it was a strange period in New York City. There was the Cotton Club where a beige beauty called Lena Horne danced to the music of the young jazz giant Duke Ellington. The club was in Harlem and the show was all black—but the audience was lily white. The bouncer would not let a black face through the door unless it belonged to an employee. In the speakeasies, the likes of Louis Armstrong could be heard playing

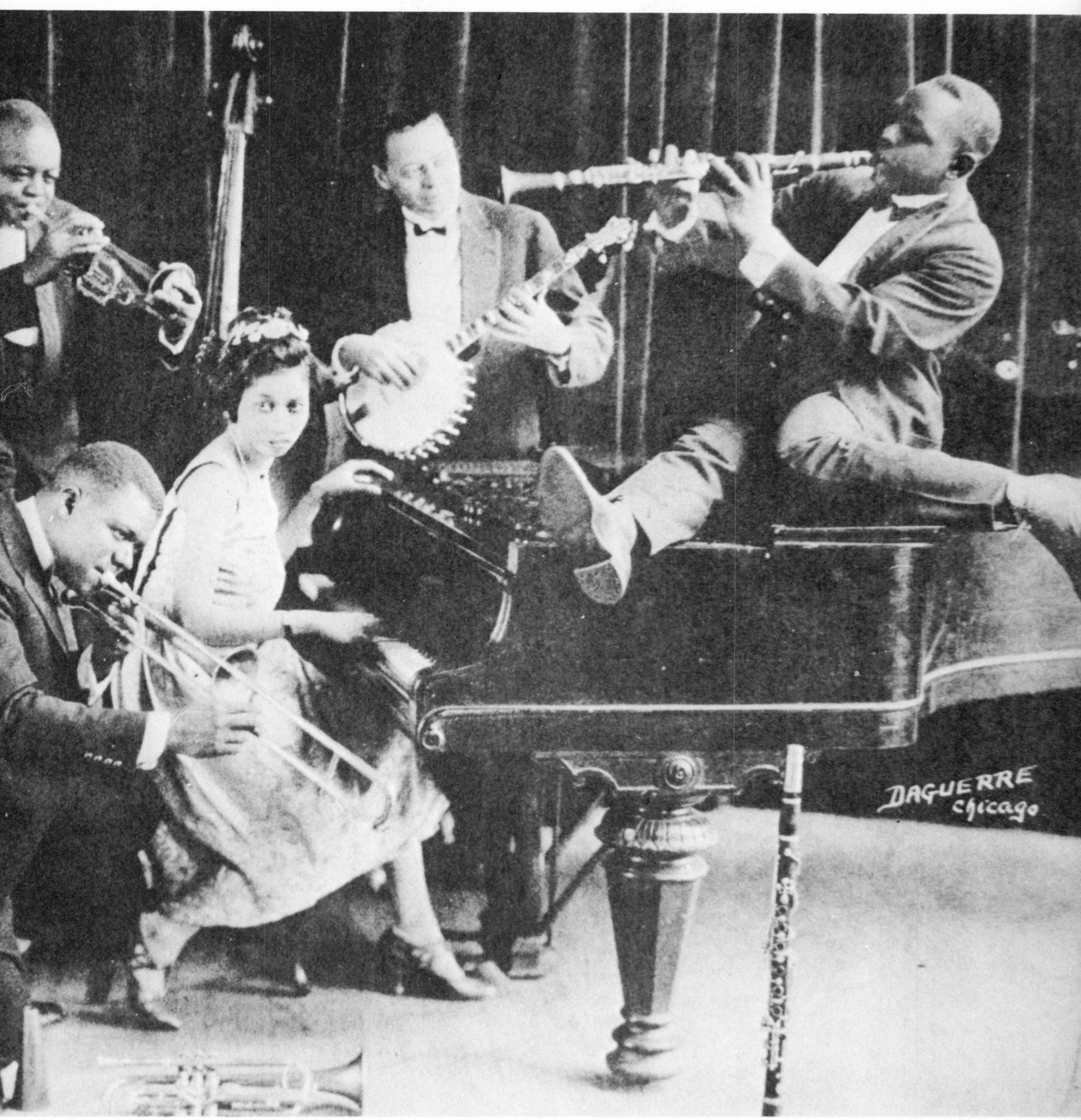

Louis Armstrong (kneeling) with King Oliver's Creole Jazz Band.

The young Edward Kennedy (Duke) Ellington became famous as a band leader and composer. He first won fame at Harlem's Cotton Club.

jazz imported from New Orleans by way of Memphis and Chicago.

In addition to Claude McKay, who wrote nonfiction and novels (including *Home To Harlem* in 1928), the giants of the Renaissance were Langston Hughes, Countee Cullen, James Weldon Johnson, Jean Toomer, W. E. B. Du Bois, Alain Locke, and Wallace Thurman.

Hughes was probably the most versatile of them all, writing poetry, short stories, plays, satire, nonfiction and drama. Born in Joplin, Missouri, Hughes had traveled to Mexico, Africa, and Europe before settling in New York. Like many young poets, he saw his first works published in *The Crisis* in the early 1920s. During the Renaissance period, Hughes published *Weary Blues*, *Fire*, and *Fine Clothes For The Jew*. His *Not Without Laughter* won him the Harmon Award for literature in 1930.

Countee Cullen was one of the few successful Harlem Renaissance writers who was born in New York City. Cullen's poetry began appearing in *The Crisis* when he was only fifteen years old. A brilliant young man, he was named Phi Beta Kappa at New York University where he was graduated in 1925 and he earned an M.A. from Harvard the next year. His first volume of poetry, *Color*, was published in 1925.

Alain Locke the philosopher and a literary critic, was close to the writers of the Harlem Renaissance period. In 1925 he published *The New Negro*, an anthology of Renaissance work. He later headed the philosophy department at Howard University. He died in 1954. His last book, *The Negro in American Culture*, was completed and published in 1956 by Margaret Butcher.

Perhaps the least prolific of the Renaissance writers was Jean Toomer, who pub-

When Dr. Ossian Sweet (r.) bought a home in Detroit in 1925, whites stoned the house and threatened Sweet and ten friends. Shots were fired and the Sweets were charged with the murder of one white man. NAACP retained the famous attorney Clarence Darrow to defend the Sweets, who were freed.

lished one book, *Cane,* in 1923 and then faded from the scene. Educated in France, Toomer wrote a series of introspective, very revealing and realistic stories of black life. His book also included some excellent poems. The book was not very well received when it was published but now it is ranked high in the literature produced during that period.

Educated at Cornell and the University of Pennsylvania, Jessie Redmond Fauset was one of the most successful female novelists of the period. *There Was Confusion* was published in 1924 and her second novel, *Plum Bun,* appeared in 1929.

James Weldon Johnson, W. E. B. Du Bois and Walter White, all executives with the NAACP, published several books during the Renaissance. Johnson's *God's Trombones* appeared in 1927. In *Black Manhattan* (1930) and *Along This Way* (1933), he told much of the story of the Harlem Renaissance.

The Harlem Renaissance did not bypass the theater. In 1919, Charles Gilpin, a product of the Lafayette Players, appeared on Broadway as the minister, William Custis, in John Drinkwater's *Abraham Lincoln* and followed it up the next year with the title role in Eugene O'Neill's *Emperor Jones.* His portrayal won him both the Drama League of New York Award and the Spingarn Medal.

Jules Bledsoe and Rose McClendon starred in Paul Green's *In Abraham's Bosom* in 1926, just two years after Paul Robeson made history in the lead role of O'Neill's *All God's Chillun Got Wings.* Robeson's appearance marked the first time a black man had played opposite a white woman on the American stage.

Elected to Congress from Chicago in 1928, Oscar DePriest (l.) became first black congressman since 1901. He is pictured with two Chicago political leaders, Louis B. Anderson (l.) and Dan Jackson.

Dorothy and DuBose Hayward's *Porgy* in 1927 and Marc Connelly's *The Green Pastures* (1930) featured black actors on Broadway.

The Renaissance period in entertainment began in 1921 with *Shuffle Along*, one of the liveliest, most brilliant musical revues New York had ever witnessed. Written and produced by four black men (F. E. Miller, Aubry Lyle, Eubie Blake and Noble Sissle), the show played New York for more than a year and then traveled on the road for two more. Two of its songs, "I'm Just Wild About Harry" and "Love Will Find A Way" became standards for years thereafter. Josephine Baker, who later became the star of the Folies Bergères in Paris, made her first appearance in New York in 1923 in Sissle and Blake's *Chocolate Dandies*. Miller and Lyle produced *Running Wild* that same year and the next year saw the debut of the fabulous Florence Mills in a revue called *Dixie To Broadway*. Miss Mills repeated her triumph in *Blackbirds of 1926*, but died in 1927. Adelaide Hall and Ada Ward starred in *Blackbirds* of 1928. Ethel Waters got her start in *Africana* in 1927 and Bill Robinson began to tap his way into the heart of America.

Musicians like writers J. Rosamond Johnson, R. Nathaniel Dett, and Harry T. Burleigh, and singers Paul Robeson, Lawrence Brown, and Roland Hayes were writing and performing for concert audiences not only in New York but around the country. Painters Aaron Douglass and Laura Wheeler Waring and sculptress Meta Warwick Fuller were winning acclaim in the arts.

It was not only in the arts that blacks displayed their ability. Biologist Ernest Everett Just, winner of the first Spingarn Medal in 1915, continued to do research and to teach brilliantly at Howard University, and historian Carter G. Woodson, director of the Association for the Study of Negro Life and History, and editor of the *Journal of Negro History*, in 1922 published *The Negro in Our History*, one of the first textbook of that kind.

While the years of the Harlem Renaissance are usually thought of as the period between 1918 and 1929, it is difficult to draw such a hard line of demarcation. It is also difficult to limit the black

Renaissance to Harlem, for many writers had begun to work even before they came to New York and there were many writers and artists of great talent who never reached the city. Let it be said that in the years following World War I, black people put their artistic talents to use and whites had to admit that black artists were more than novelties.

Jesse Binga (above) built a strong bank in Chicago. The bank failed during Depression.

6

Depression

The year 1929 started inauspiciously enough. Republican Herbert Hoover was inaugurated president after a mild upset over Alfred E. Smith, the smiling Democrat from New York. Hoover was the first modern Republican presidential candidate to make an open bid for the white South, and black Republicans and knowledgeable Northern Republicans saw the handwriting on the wall. The white South was taking away representation at the Republican National Convention which traditionally had gone to black Southern Republicans such as Perry Howard of Mississippi, Benjamin Davis of Georgia, and Robert Church of Tennessee. The move had paid off for Hoover, who carried Florida, Kentucky, North Carolina, Texas, Virginia, and West Virginia. Al Smith was a Roman Catholic and his religion cost him support in the South, so white Republicans could not claim all the credit for Hoover's strength in traditionally Democratic states.

In his inaugural address, President Hoover stated that he would be president of all the people and he called for law and order in a speech which anticipated the address made by Republican President Richard M. Nixon some forty years later. "The most malign of all dangers today," said Hoover, "is disregard and disobedience of law. . . . Our whole system of self-government will crumble if officials elect what laws they will enforce or citizens elect what laws they will support. . . . If citizens do not like a law their duty as honest men and women is openly to work for its repeal."

Congressman Oscar DePriest (R., Ill.) took office that year and told his fellow blacks, "You will never get what you want politically unless you will elect leaders who will fight for your interest. . . . Don't complain about racial discrimination. Change it by practical politics." DePriest was addressing a rally at New York's Abyssinian Baptist Church where Adam Clayton Powell Sr. was then pastor and whose members were later to help elect Adam Clayton Powell Jr. first to the city council and then to Congress.

That year the sixth annual convention of Marcus Garvey's UNIA was held in Kingston, Jamaica, and in New York City the Urban League organized a "Jobs For Negroes" movement to boycott white businesses which made their money from black people but did not employ them.

Down in Atlanta, a baby was born who was baptized Martin Luther King Jr. and in Detroit, John Conyers Jr., later to sit in Congress, first saw the light of day.

In New York, Micheaux Pictures Company, a black-owned firm, was producing Negro movies and Fox movie company released the first black talkie, *Hearts of Dixie,* starring Stepin Fetchit as a shuffling comedian. King Vidor produced the movie *Hallelujah* with an all-black cast.

In New York City, Richard B. Harrison won acclaim for his portrayal of De Lawd in white writer Marc Connelly's allegorical play, *Green Pastures.*

But despite all this, there were no green pastures for black people in 1929. When the stock market crashed in October, whites were caught by surprise but black people had been feeling the pinch for several years.

The plight of black banking institutions was one of the first indicators. In the early

Headlines in *The New York Times* in October, 1929, showed bankers' optimism in the face of financial disintegration.

WORST STOCK CRASH STEMMED BY BANKS; 12,894,650-SHARE DAY SWAMPS MARKET; LEADERS CONFER, FIND CONDITIONS SOUND

FINANCIERS EASE TENSION

Five Wall Street Bankers Hold Two Meetings at Morgan Office.

Wall Street Optimistic After Stormy Day; Clerical Work May Force Holiday Tomorrow

Confidence in the soundness of the stock market structure, notwithstanding the upheaval of the last few days, was voiced last night by bankers and other financial leaders. Sentiment as expressed by the heads of some of the largest banking institutions and by industrial executives as well was distinctly cheerful and the feeling was general that the worst had been seen. Wall Street ended the day in an optimistic frame of mind.

LOSSES RECOVERED IN PART

Upward Trend Start With 200,000-Share Order for Steel.

From "The New York Times," October 25, 1929.

STOCK PRICES SLUMP $14,000,000,000 IN NATION-WIDE STAMPEDE TO UNLOAD; BANKERS TO SUPPORT MARKET TODAY

Sixteen Leading Issues Down $2,893,520,108; Tel. & Tel. and Steel Among Heaviest Losers

PREMIER ISSUES HARD HIT

From "The New York Times," October 29, 1929.

STOCKS COLLAPSE IN 16,410,030-SHARE DAY, BUT RALLY AT CLOSE CHEERS BROKERS; BANKERS OPTIMISTIC, TO CONTINUE AID

LEADERS SEE FEAR WANING

Point to 'Lifting Spells' in Trading as Sign of Buying Activity.

GROUP MEETS TWICE IN DAY

240 Issues Lose $15,894,818,894 in Month; Slump in Full Exchange List Vastly Larger

The drastic effects of Wall Street's October bear market is shown by valuation tables prepared last night by THE NEW YORK TIMES, which place the decline in the market value of 240 representative issues on the New York Stock Exchange at $15,894,818,894 during the period from Oct. 1 to yesterday's closing. Since there are 1,279 issues listed on the New York Stock Exchange, the total depreciation for the month is estimated at between two and three times the loss for the 240 issues covered by THE TIMES table.

Among the losses of the various groups comprising the 240 stocks in THE TIMES valuation table were the following:

CLOSING RALLY VIGOROUS

Leading Issues Regain From 4 to 14 Points in 15 Minutes.

INVESTMENT TRUSTS BUY

From "The New York Times," October 30, 1929.

1920s there were some thirty black banks in the United States and in 1926 they had total resources of some $13 million. These banks began to decline in 1927, faded more rapidly after 1929 and, by 1931, their resources had dropped to $7 million. Even before the Depression, more than half of the black banks failed.

While poor personal management caused some of the failures, most were attributed to the character of business in black neighborhoods: recreational and amusement establishments (theaters, clubs, pool rooms, etc.), real estate, retail trade and personal service businesses (barber shops, beauty parlors, dry cleaners, etc.). These businesses are responsive to the state of income of their customers. When a man loses his job or is cut back on the number of hours he works, he cuts personal services sharply, economizes on his retail buying—even of food—and is not in the market for purchasing a home or moving to a more expensive apartment. Ghetto businesses are immediately affected, and banks are hit in two ways—the unemployed man withdraws his savings and is slow to repay loans, and black businesses reduce their use of the banks. The banks do not have sufficient long-term deposits and may even have to foreclose on homes for nonpayments of mortgages. They then own property for which there is no market. Marginal businesses fail and the ghetto is in trouble long before the rest of the nation.

The Great Depression came as a sudden tragedy, especially to wealthy whites and those of the middle class who were trying to "get rich quick" in the stock market. The stock market crash came because stocks were bought at highly inflated prices on borrowed money (on margin) for which the value of the stock itself was the only collateral. When the stock fell to its true worth or even below, speculators found themselves in debt for hundreds of thousands, some even millions, of dollars.

Very few blacks were involved in the stock market crash for very few blacks were involved in the stock market anyway. For blacks and poor whites the blow was more indirect. As more and more factories either failed or cut back on production, black men, "the last hired and the first fired," joined the ranks of the unemployed. Black women who worked as domestics for the wealthy whites lost their jobs as the whites lost their money. Unemployment for the country skyrocketed and, particularly for black men in the North, the results were disastrous.

In Detroit in 1931, 60 percent of black workers were unemployed as compared with 32 percent of whites. In Houston, Texas, 35 percent of black workers and 18 percent of white workers were unemployed. As late as 1937, unemployment figures for workers in the North showed 38.9 percent of black men unemployed as

At Los Angeles Central Produce Terminal, jobless men and women search for food in garbage cans and carry away scraps of wood to burn in poverty-stricken homes.

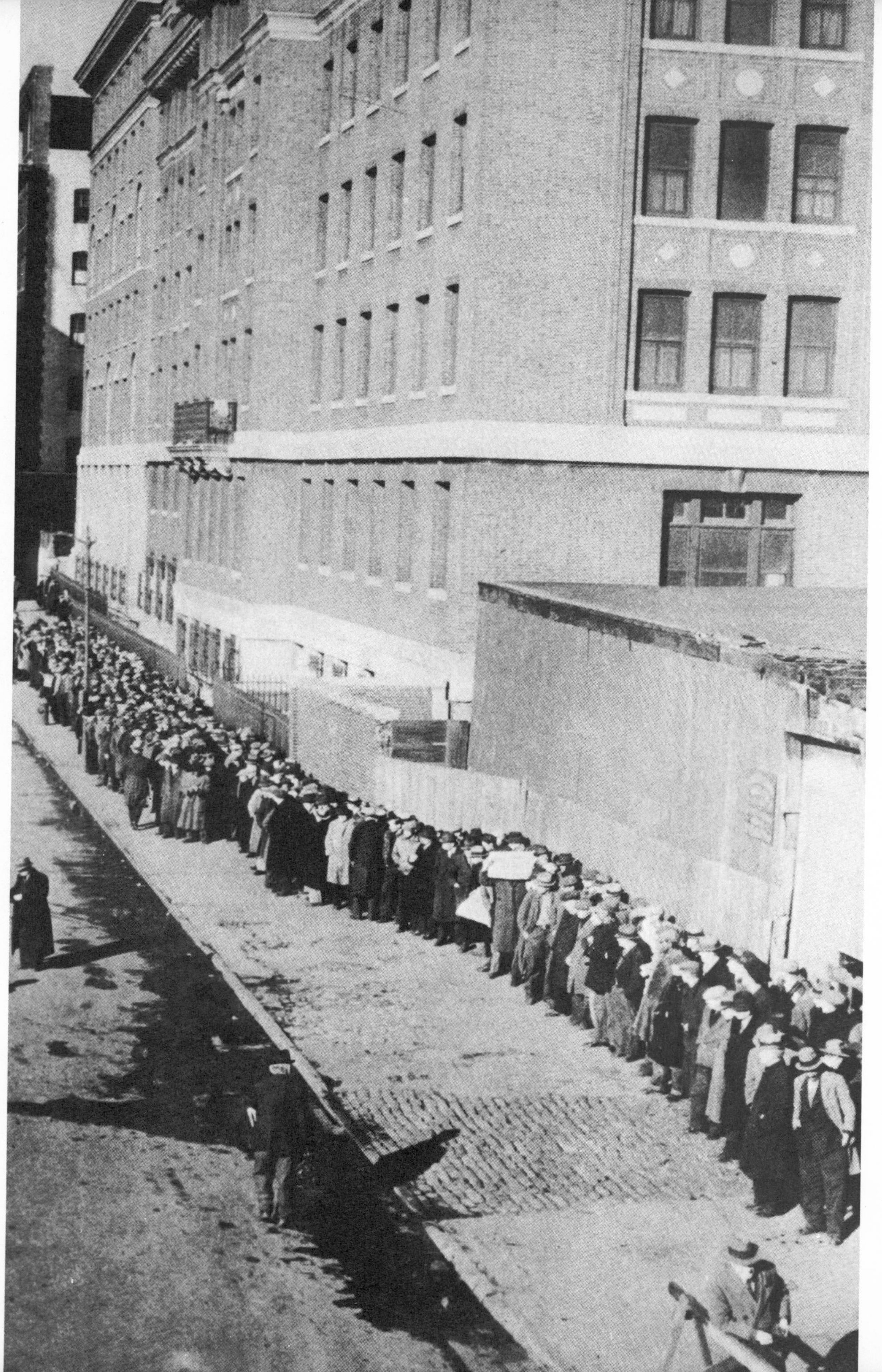

opposed to only 18.1 percent among whites. In the South, where most blacks worked in agriculture, the difference was much less. Unemployment for blacks was 18 percent and for whites, 16 percent. For black and white women in the North, the figures paralleled those of the men. Black

"Breadlines" of unemployed wait for food handouts (left) and children in Harlem receive food from Catholic nuns (above).

women were unemployed at a rate of 42.9 percent while the figure for whites was 26.2 percent. The only place and category where blacks had slightly the best of it was for black women in the South whose unemployment rate of 26 percent was a hair better than the 26.2 percent figure for white women.

The misery among black people during

the Depression was a misery of number and degree. Black folk since slavery had learned to cope with misery and the recent migrations of rural Southern blacks to urban ghettos had provided a good training course in enduring a Depression. Packed into ghettos at a density three and four times the buildings were meant to house, lacking sufficient conveniences (sometimes only one bath to four floors), with whole families crowded into one room and three or four families sharing a single kitchen, blacks, even before the Depression, went through misery as they learned to adjust to an urban life and Northern discrimination. On the way up, most had, at one time or another, to depend upon the charity of friends or relatives or "go on welfare" in order to survive.

As the Depression continued, black families turned to relief in vast numbers. In Northern cities where there was little discrimination in granting relief, 52.2 percent of all black families were drawing government aid. In urban areas of the South black families on relief ranged from 22 to 46 percent of the total black families, from four to seven times the rate for whites. But whites were granted higher payments, averaging $29.05 as opposed to $24.18 for black families. In the rural South a greater percentage of white families drew relief payments.

It was in the big cities, particularly in the big cities of the North, that blacks were most affected by the Depression. They met the new challenge with the same style that had helped them survive slavery, Reconstruction, discrimination, segregation, and migration. In New York,

Cotton crops and prices slumped but some blacks in the South continued to work at near-starvation wages.

The unemployed organized hunger marches (above) to stress their plight. As late as 1939 blacks were demonstrating (right) against the security wage provisions of the WPA.

Chicago, Detroit, Philadelphia, and other cities with a sizable black population, life went on. During the 1920s, Harlem had developed a peculiar innovation of survival called the "house rent party." The biggest ogre in the slums was the landlord who had to be paid (weekly or monthly) if one wanted to continue to have a roof over one's head. Apartment dwellers would periodically clear out a room of furniture, leaving only a battered piano, to make room for dancing. In the kitchen there would be a pot of chitlins and another of pig feet. Perhaps there would be greens and black eyed peas. Corn whiskey or bathtub gin or home brewed beer would be made available. Everybody got ready for a party but with a new twist. Anyone who paid the charge of 15 cents at the door was welcome. The chitlins, pig feet, gin, whiskey, and beer were all for sale.

During the Depression, rent parties spread to most Northern black ghettos. It was the black man's neighborly way of helping his brother survive.

The rent party became such a favorite in Chicago that it provided work and exposure for gutbucket piano players who eventually found their way to small clubs and taverns as entertainers after the repeal of Prohibition.

In major cities, poor black folk had to have something that gave them the promise of surcease from the constant struggle for existence. Whites looked to an inheritance from a wealthy relative or from a killing on the stock market (before the crash). To the black man, the hope lay in "hitting the number" (in the East) or "hitting policy" (in the Midwest). Both numbers and policy, though winners were arrived at differently, had one thing in common—for a small play you could win at tremendous odds. Ignored by most was the fact that there were also tremendous odds against winning at all. At any rate, men, women and even children played numbers and policy and every so often someone in the neighborhood would hit it big enough to keep the hopes of others alive. In the East, in New York City, Philadelphia, Washington, and Baltimore, the numbers game was controlled by white gangsters; but in Chicago, for a long time, policy, with its independent

wheels and its local backing, was controlled by black policy barons who were usually men of some standing in the community. Few blacks considered policy illegal. The Jones brothers, George and Ed, controlled policy and became millionaires in Chicago before the syndicate realized how much money there was in the nickel-and-dime game and took it over, forcing the Jones brothers to move to Mexico.

Black folk could live without money and sometimes it seemed as if they could live without food or shelter but they could not live without hope. For those who did not take the numbers road to hope (and some who did) there was another road, and that was through the church. It didn't have to be a big or a rich church. It just had to be a church that held out hope. In Chicago in the 1930s some fifty-five store front churches were spaced along South State Street between Twenty-second and Fifty-third streets. The small, independent churches were also popular in New York, Philadelphia, and other major cities. Sometimes a dynamic store-front church preacher would attract such a large and devoted following that his congregation would build an imposing edifice and the church would become a powerful factor

Young city dwellers were recruited for the Civilian Conservation Corps and sent to work in government forestry projects.

A WPA writers' project sit-in in New York City (left) discussed mass action in San Francisco (above) to protest a 40 percent layoff in 1936.

in the community. Examples of this were The First Church of Deliverance pastored by the Reverend Clarence Cobbs and the Cosmopolitan Church of the Reverend Mary Evans, both on Wabash Avenue on Chicago's South Side.

Occasionally, a "store-front" minister, quiet and undistinguished in appearance and yet possessing a strange charisma that led others to follow him, would become a veritable messiah to many. One such man was George Baker, a short, dark, rather stocky man with no apparent attractions. He is said to have been born near Savannah, Georgia, and, in the late 1890s, opened his first church. Calling himself the "Son of Righteousness," Baker is said to have left town just ahead of a group of white hoodlums who were intent upon making him prove he could walk on water. Baker then turned up in Baltimore where, supposedly inspired by a preacher called Father Jehovia, he began to think of himself as divine. Gathering unto himself twelve apostles, six male and six female, he toured the South as an evangelist. Finally, in 1915, he moved to Brooklyn, New York, where he set up a small religious commune. Adopting the name Major Morgan J. Divine, he lived in Brooklyn for about four years. In 1919, he bought an eight-room house in suburban Sayville, Long Island, and obtained a license to operate an employment agency which would supply black domestic help to the well-to-do whites who made up the bulk of Sayville's population. Divine had a small group of followers who lived at his "mission." The leader provided the whites with domestic help and each Sunday he held services which were followed by huge banquets which were free to all comers. By the time the Depression started, Divine was an institution in Sayville. He drew no color line and the good white folk of Sayville began to be upset because of the large interracial crowds attracted to the small town. Eventually, Divine was arrested and tried for maintaining a public nuisance. He was found guilty and sentenced to serve one year in

Langdon W. Post, chairman of New York Housing Authority, accepted a low income housing project built by Public Works Administration in 1934. About 34 percent of housing projects were for poor blacks.

President Franklin Delano Roosevelt made history by appointing blacks to responsible government posts. His "black cabinet" (above) included one woman, Mary McLeod Bethune.

jail. The judge, Lewis J. Smith, is supposed to have called Divine a "menace to society." Divine reportedly answered, "Pity the judge, he can't live long. He has offended Almighty God." Judge Smith dropped dead four days later. Legend has it that in his cell, Divine said, "I hated to do it." From then on, the minister used the name Father Divine and his followers said, "Father Divine is God." There is no record that Divine ever made that claim for himself. Newspapers, both black and white, told the story of the black man in Sayville who predicted a judge's death. Divine appealed his public nuisance case and his conviction was reversed. Father Divine then sold his mission in Sayville for a substantial profit and moved his flock to a Turkish bathhouse he had purchased as a "Heaven" for his followers. His converts, most of them women although there were a number of men, could live in the "Heaven," though the sexes were carefully segregated, getting together for the services, religious dancing and singing, and for the weekly banquet. In a time of economic depression, when small businesses were failing, the followers of Father Divine began opening grocery stores, laundries, barber shops, and restaurants. The shops doubled as Father Divine missions or churches. He next started a newspaper (*The New Day*) and a magazine (*The Spoken Word*) so that he could stay in communication with his followers. Father Divine's Peace Mission movement began growing as rapidly as had Marcus Garvey's Universal Negro Improvement Association. There was little friction within the movement even though it was interracial. A white man, Brother Lamb, was one of the leading disciples as public relations man and a business manager.

The movement soon began to expand beyond New York City. There were missions and "Heavens" as far west as Los Angeles and throughout the South. The Divine restaurants were very successful. For a dime one could purchase a full meal of wholesome, well-prepared food. The

President Roosevelt invited leaders of black fraternal groups like Masons and Elks to meet with him in the White House.

Arthur W. Mitchell defeated Oscar DePriest for a seat in Congress in 1934. The Chicago Democrat served until 1942.

restaurants were open to the public and customers did not have to profess a belief in the divinity of Father Divine in order to eat there. It was usually true, however, that waitresses (usually matronly ladies) greeted with the slogan, "Peace, it's truly wonderful," would be likely to put an extra yam on the diner's plate.

Father Divine's enterprises prospered for several reasons. The "angels" were not paid for their work and no taxes had to be paid because the businesses were run for a religious organization. The businesses were successful for yet another reason—all followers of Father Divine were scrupulously honest and well-mannered. They consistently gave full measure and full quality.

Mary McLeod Bethune and Eleanor Roosevelt became close friends (left). Mrs. Bethune was a frequent visitor at the White House.

EAT

Father Divine's Peace Mission movement was so successful that he was able to purchase property at Krum Elbow across the river from President Roosevelt's estate in New York. He was also able to buy a $1 million hotel in Atlantic City, and city and country "Heavens" in Philadelphia when he fell out of favor with the authorities in New York City. His movement survived his marriage to a young white woman in his declining years. Even after his death in 1965 his cult continued to exist though not on the scale of the thirties and forties.

The Peace Mission movement and the International Righteous Government of Father Divine came along at a time when he served the needs of thousands of poor people. In a time of Depression, he offered them the security of food to eat and a roof over their heads. He also gave them a sense of "belonging" and of knowing that someone cared for them. Father Divine's followers were seldom in trouble with the law and never went on relief. Many gamblers, thieves, and prostitutes joined a "Heaven" and reformed. It is said that Father Divine attracted many who had once followed Marcus Garvey, and in his later years Garvey was to talk of the cultist who tried to steal his followers.

Father Divine was not the only cultist to achieve national fame during the Depression. In Washington, D.C., Elder Solomon Lightfoot Michaux built a huge following as the "Happy Am I" minister whose Sunday services went out to hundreds of thousands on radio. The singing, clapping, swinging rhythms of his services reached both blacks and whites and money came into his coffers from many surrounding states. Elder Michaux founded the Good Neighbor League in Washington. In 1933 the organization is said to have fed some 250,000 poor people free of charge in its Happy News Cafe. Michaux became involved in politics, supporting Franklin D. Roosevelt. He later used his Good Neighbor League to help organize the black vote for Roosevelt.

At one time Father Divine, too, became involved in politics. Through his International Righteous Government division he supported Fiorello H. LaGuardia for mayor of New York City and Roosevelt for president of the United States. He also

Nine black youths were saved from lynching (left) by National Guard when they were accused of raping two white women near Scottsboro, Alabama. The trial of the "Scottsboro Boys" was a major event of the thirties. Defense attorney Samuel Leibowitz and others eventually won freedom for the men.

made appeals for the release of Angelo Herndon, a young black Communist who was being held in prison in Atlanta. Divine's interest in politics stopped almost as abruptly as it started and he vowed never to get involved again. No one knows why.

Another cultist who was a success primarily on the East Coast (New York, Philadelphia, Baltimore, and Washington) was "Sweet Daddy" Grace, an imposing minister who attempted at one time to steal Father Divine's following but with very little success. A flamboyant spiritualist who let his fingernails grow long to show that he did not have to work with his hands, Daddy Grace preached well and had a knack of getting people to

Rev. George Baker, famous as cult leader Father Divine, won a court victory (above) after being charged with boarding children without a permit. Below, he enters his car in Philadelphia.

part with their money. Unfortunately, he gave his followers little in return, except spiritual fulfillment, and he could not compete with Father Divine's free board and room programs.

For those who preferred more secular entertainment, there was abundant choice. The 1930s were a time of big band jazz and swing, when probably more beautiful ballads were written than in any other decade in American history. Fletcher Henderson's band had come up in the twenties and was in full swing by the thirties. The jumping jazz of Louis Armstrong, Louis Jordan, Cab Calloway, and Count Basie was at its uninhibited best, and the sophisticated "swing" of Jimmie Lunceford, Noble Sissle, and Duke Ellington was beginning to win national acclaim. It was a time of glory for black musicians. Black dance bands, singers, and dancers were in vogue. In fact, one of the biggest hits at the 1939 World's Fair in New York was Billy Rose's popular production of Gilbert and Sullivan's *Mikado* featuring top Negro musicians. In Harlem, black-owned Small's Paradise presented excellent revues and the best of black musicians. In Chicago the Club DeLisa, The Grand Terrace, and Swingland were the top spots for black entertainment. In New York, people paid the price of admission just to watch the dancers at the Savoy Ballroom, "The Home of Happy Feet." Rug-cutting, Susie Q-ing, and Lindy Hopping were exciting spectator entertainment.

In sports, in the early Depression, blacks had little to cheer about. Baseball and professional football were closed to blacks. There were few blacks on major college football teams (Kenny Washington starred at UCLA and Ozzie Simmons was at the University of Iowa). There were no black contenders for the heavyweight boxing crown, but John Henry Lewis was the top light heavyweight (He won the title in 1935.)

But memorable things were to happen in sports during the Depression. Strangely, four of the most important sports events of the decade had international overtones.

For the first, go to the night of June 25, 1935. Out in Yankee Stadium, a young boxer named Joe Louis, relatively unknown at this time and not yet a hero, even to blacks, was fighting Primo Carnera. Joe Louis was out of the Alabama cottonfields by way of the assembly line at the Ford Motor Company plant in Detroit. He had had a brilliant amateur career and was moving forward now as a professional. He had black managers, Julian Black and John Roxborough, and a black trainer, Jack Blackburn. Carnera was the giant Italian brought over to stimulate the fight game. Carnera was six feet five and he weighed more than 260 pounds. Italy was at war with Ethiopia and Emperor Haile Selassie was trying to enlist the aid of black people all over the world in his cause. Blacks were afraid that if Carnera defeated Louis, the fight would provide the Italians with more fodder for propaganda. Blacks desperately wanted a big victory for Louis, but they had no guarantee that he could even win, let alone win decisively. In six rounds Louis pummeled and cut his huge opponent down to size. Carnera was felled three times and in the sixth round the referee stopped the fight. Immediately Joe Louis became a race hero—a source of pride to all black men.

Just a year later, Louis was back in Yankee Stadium, after four more victories, to fight Max Schmeling. Schmeling was a German, and Germany was under the rule of Aryan master race theorist Adolf Hitler. The publicity made this a grudge fight—the Aryan hero against "the inferior black." If blacks had been writing the script, Louis would have knocked out Schmeling. But Schmeling refused to follow that script. Finding a flaw in Louis's defense, Schmeling pounded punch after punch into Louis's body and finally knocked him out in the twelfth round.

Louis's loss was a bitter blow to black people all over the world as well as to whites who opposed the theories of racial supremacy preached by Adolf Hitler. New York's Harlem and the "Harlems" of the world were cast into deep despair. Blacks cried, fought and drank to hide their sorrows. And then they said that the next time things would be different.

But the year had one redeeming feature. The 1936 Olympic Games were held in Germany; and two months after Louis's defeat, on a day when Hitler was in the stands, Jesse Owens, then the world's fastest human, took gold medals in both the 100- and 200-meter dashes—setting an Olympic record in the 200. It is said that Hitler left the stadium early to avoid having to formally congratulate the black

Father Divine visits his Krum Elbow "Heaven" across the Hudson River from President Roosevelt's Hyde Park home.

athlete. Owens also set a world and Olympic record in the running broad jump and anchored the 400-meter relay team to world record victory. It was one of the greatest Olympic performances ever and the fact that it took place in Hitler's Berlin made it all the more satisfying.

After losing to Schmeling, Joe Louis knocked out seven successive opponents to win a chance at the heavyweight crown worn by aging James J. Braddock. Louis knocked out Braddock in the eighth round to become heavyweight champion on June 22, 1937. He now had but one aim—a return bout with Schmeling.

Some seventy thousand spectators crowded Yankee Stadium, including one thousand Germans who had come to the U.S. to attend this fight. A confident Schmeling talked of Aryan superiority. Louis said nothing.

The entire world was at fever pitch over this fight. There was no television in those

The NAACP was the strongest civil rights organization in the 1930s. Under the leadership of Walter White (above) and the legal guidance of Charles H. Houston (below), the association won many victories.

days, and people poured into the city by bus, car, train, and plane. Betting was brisk with Louis a slight favorite.

It is said that this was the only time that the usually good-natured Joe Louis entered the ring with hatred in his heart. Schmeling had not only humiliated him, he had continued to talk about his victory and about Aryan supremacy.

At the sound of the first bell Joe shuffled quickly to the attack. Then he exploded. His blows flew so fast that even ringsiders could not keep track of them. Battered from body to head and back to body again, Schmeling went down three times in the first round and the fight was over. It is said that Schmeling threw only four punches in the entire fight.

The victory was the answer to the black man's prayers. There was dancing in the streets of Harlem that night. The hero had returned and black men could again hold up their heads.

The NAACP and other civil rights organizations, both black and white, kept up a steady protest against the brutal practice of lynching during the days of the Depression. In 1929, Walter White's book, *Rope And Faggot, A Biography of Judge Lynch,* based on his ten-year study of lynching, was published. The very next year, twenty blacks were lynched and in 1931 another twelve met death at the hands of mobs. Six Negroes were lynched in 1932, twenty-four in 1933, fifteen in 1934, eighteen in 1935, eight in 1936, eight in 1937, six in 1938, two in 1939 and four in 1940. Southern congressmen continued to foil any attempt to pass an antilynch bill.

While the NAACP continued the fight against lynching, the Urban League launched a campaign to get more jobs for blacks—particularly in businesses where much of the trade was black. The local Urban Leagues organized boycotts of stores in St. Louis and Chicago which

would not hire black clerks as early as 1927. The Jobs-For-Negroes campaigns spread widely throughout the nation and their slogan became, "Don't Buy Where You Can't Work." The *Pittsburgh Courier* organized a Negro Housewives League to demonstrate the buying power of blacks. In Chicago, the aggressive weekly newspaper, the *Whip*, and the Reverend J. C. Austin of Pilgrim Baptist Church organized the Illinois Civic Association and won the backing of almost the entire South Side in boycotts of department stores, bakeries, breweries, and dairies. In New York, the Citizens' League For Fair Play was organized by another newspaper-church combination, this time the Reverend John H. Johnson, rector of St. Martin's Episcopal Church, and Fred R. Moore, editor and publisher of the *New York Age*. The Citizens' League tried persuasion and finally boycotts to win jobs for blacks.

Because of the misery and turmoil among blacks in the ghettos, home-grown Communists made another attempt to win black support. Where they had once tried to woo the black intellectual, they now wanted to show that they were the champions of the underdog. There had been a people's revolt in Russia during World War I and the proletariat had won. Now, about a dozen years later, Russia seemed one of the more stable countries in the world, for most of the western nations were in the throes of a depression.

The Communists needed a *cause cèlèbre* and they were handed one ready-made by the state of Alabama in 1931. Hoboing from Chattanooga to Memphis on a freight train on March 25, a group of white and black youths got into a fight and five whites were thrown off the train near Stevenson, Alabama. The white youths then told white residents that the

Lloyd Gaines won the right to be admitted to University of Missouri Law School with the 1938 Supreme Court ruling that the state must provide equal education "within the state" for all citizens. After winning the case, Gaines disappeared from his room (left) in Alpha House in Chicago. He has not been heard from since.

FRAGER

blacks had two white girls on the train and word was sent ahead to Paint Rock, Alabama, where an angry posse was waiting. The black youths fled but nine were rounded up and charged with the rape of the two white women, Victoria Price and Nancy Bates, who were on the train. On the testimony of the two women, the nine youths were tried and found guilty. Andy Wright, Haywood Patterson, Eugene Williams, Clarence Norris, Charles Weems, Ozzie Powell, Willie Roberson and Olen Montgomery were sentenced to death and Roy White to life in prison. The International Labor Defense, a Communist party organ, heard about the case and wanted to step in. About the same time, the NAACP was notified and wanted to take over the defense of the youths. The tale is that the ILD attacked the NAACP in talks with the parents of the boys and convinced them that the ILD should be retained to represent the youths. The ILD organized a world-wide protest, sending the mother of Andy Wright on a tour abroad where she led demonstrations in twenty-eight countries. American embassies were stoned and picketed and hundreds of letters were written to President Hoover and to the governor of Alabama. The Communists are said to have raised $1 million for the defense of the "Scottsboro Boys" and the noted New York lawyer Samuel Liebowitz was retained to handle the case. On November 7, 1932, the United States Supreme Court ordered a new trial.

By 1933 it had been established that the two women on the train had questionable reputations and Nancy Bates withdrew her testimony. Proof of rape could not be established, but the new jury, on April 17, 1933, again found the defendants guilty. The judge hearing the case was so incensed at the jury's verdict that he wrote

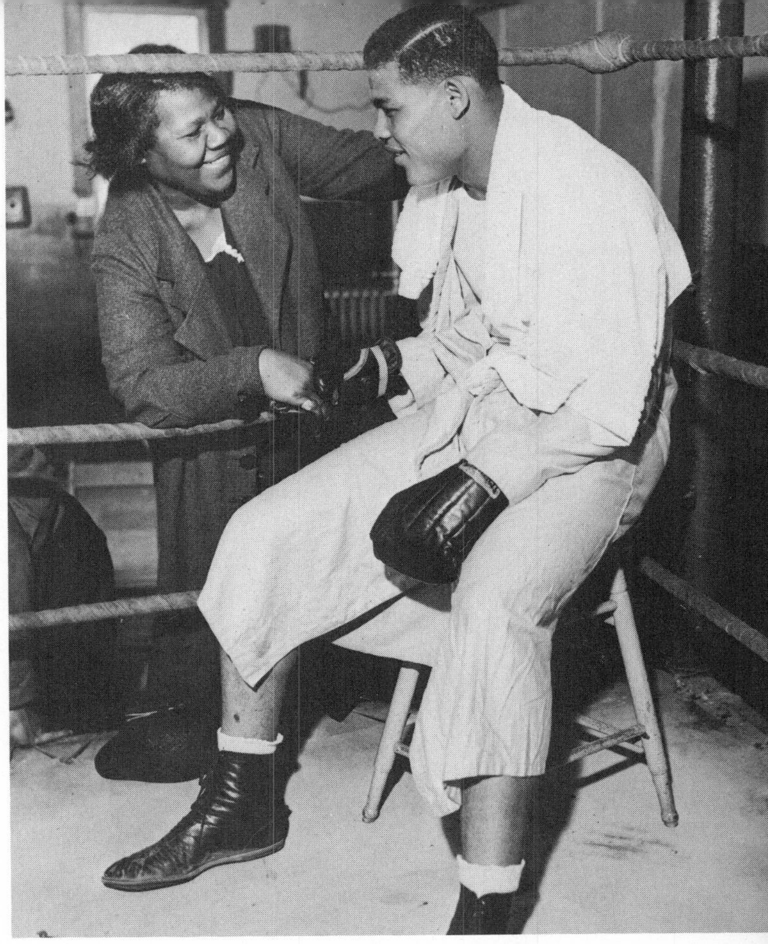

In 1937 folk hero Joe Louis, seen here with his mother, Mrs. Lillian B. Brooks, became the first black heavyweight champion since Jack Johnson. He k.o.'d Max Schmeling in 1938.

Famous painting by George Bellows (above) shows Louis knocking out Schmeling. Opposite page, Louis's hand is raised in victory after his defeat of James Braddock at Comiskey Park in 1937.

a brief condemning it and immediately granted the defense a new trial. At the third trial, in November, 1933, the youths were again found guilty. The case was taken to the Supreme Court and on April 1, 1935, the convictions were reversed with the court stating that a fair trial was denied the defendants because Negroes were excluded from the jury. New warrants were sworn out by Victoria Price and a grand jury returned new indictments for rape. In December, 1935, the Scottsboro Defense Committee was

formed, this time with the NAACP, the American Civil Liberties Union, the League for Industrial Democracy and the Episcopal Federation for Social Service joining forces with the ILD. The National Urban League was an unofficial member of the defense committee. Joining Liebowitz were lawyer Allan Chalmers, and C. I. Watts, a local lawyer from Huntsville, Alabama. The fight to save the Scottsboro Boys went on until the ninth man was finally freed in 1950. Earlier, the state had made a deal to release four men and try five for assault. Instead, they sentenced Norris to death and sentenced the other four to terms ranging from twenty to ninety-five years.

The committee continued working on the governor and the pardon board and, by 1948, three more were free. That year Haywood Patterson escaped to Detroit and the governor refused to extradite him. Patterson wrote a book, *Scottsboro Boy*, which told of the horrors of prisons in the South. The case lasted nineteen years and it is one of the most famous in history.

The furor raised by the Communists over the Scottsboro Boys showed that they could be effective but, though some blacks flirted with the leftist movement, few embraced Communism, even though the Communists usually ran at least one black man on their ticket in national elections, slating James Ford as the vice-presidential candidate in 1932, 1936, and 1940.

The NAACP put up the bulk of the money for the latter part of the fight to save the Scottsboro Boys and more and more the organization found itself moving

into the courts to advance the cause of justice for black people.

That the NAACP could afford to go to law, an expensive procedure at any time, during the Depression was largely due to the eccentricity of a young white man who refused an inheritance of more than a million dollars.

Charles Garland was the man who declined a fortune, deciding instead to organize the American Fund For Public Service. He turned the huge inheritance over to the fund with the request that the money be given away as quickly as possible to aid "unpopular causes" without regard to race, creed, or color.

Jesse Owens set a world record in the broad jump (above), and went to the victory stand (below) four times in 1936 in the Berlin Olympics. He also won the 100- and 200-meter dashes and was a member of the world-record-setting 400-meter relay team.

Included in the unpopular causes aided by Charles Garland's inheritance were the Urban League, The Brotherhood of Sleeping Car Porters, and the NAACP. The NAACP decided to use its share of the money to step up the fight for court decisions that would have the same widespread effect among blacks as its Supreme Court victories banning the "Grandfather Clause," residential segregation, the Texas primary law, and jury trials in an atmosphere of mob pressure.

Charles Hamilton Houston, an Amherst and Harvard graduate and a vice dean at Howard University, was hired as the special counsel of the NAACP. Aided by

Ralph Metcalfe ran in the 1936 Olympics. Metcalfe was a member of the winning 400-meter relay team. In the picture above, Metcalfe is talking with German athletes.

Barred from major league baseball, black ballplayers established their own leagues and developed their own star players, among them Satchel Paige and Josh Gibson.

Dancer Bill (Bojangles) Robinson appeared with singer Adelaide Hall in her last performance before moving to London.

Thurgood Marshall and William Henry Hastie, Houston mounted a campaign to open graduate schools in the South to black students. Other aims were the reorganization of the NAACP into two divisions, the civil rights arm of the main body which could take political action, and the Legal Defense Fund, which could become a not-for-profit legal agency defending the rights of the poor and helpless. Thurgood Marshall, student and protégé of Houston, eventually succeeded him and carried on the work until his appointment in 1967 as the first black man on the United States Supreme Court.

BLACK AMERICANS, the stepchildren of the world's largest democracy, seem to profit from major calamities. There is no doubt that World War I, in the long run, benefited the black man. It speeded his movement out of the South, opened up a whole new job world to him, gave his women their first opportunity for industrial training and work.

Like World War I, the Great Depression led to some black gains. First of all, through Roosevelt, it gave the black man a reason for breaking away from the Republican party, which had not done anything for him since the Civil War. To be sure, Roosevelt wasn't concerned particularly with black folk. But he was committed to pulling the country out of a Depression, which made it necessary for him to help blacks.

When Franklin Delano Roosevelt was first elected president in 1932, it was not the black vote which put him in office. It is true that he attracted more black votes than any recent Democratic candidate but blacks, though disenchanted with the Republican party, were not ready to go for the party of the Bilbos and Longs of the South. Roosevelt soon won the trust of the

Bill Robinson tap-danced his way to the top of the entertainment world during the Depression.

Hattie McDaniel, a character actress, was the first black to win an Academy Award—best supporting actress for her role in *Gone With The Wind* in 1940.

black man who not only appreciated what the president was doing but also liked the style with which he did it.

FDR took office in March, 1933, with a national banking crisis on his hands. Roosevelt closed the banks, reorganized regulations to guarantee the savings of the little man, and then went on radio to talk to the people before the banks were reopened. He so reassured them that when the bank holiday ended, people rushed to the banks to put their money back in.

Savoy Ballroom, "The Home Of Happy Feet," was a top tourist attraction in Harlem.

Big bands like Erskine Hawkins' were popular during the Depression. Dancing to name bands was a popular recreation of the period.

Fletcher Henderson

Jimmy Lunceford

Andy Kirk

Thomas (Fats) Waller, a leading jazz pianist and composer, was the son of a minister. He wrote the hits, "Ain't Misbehavin' " and "Honeysuckle Rose."

Roosevelt knew little about black people before his involvement in politics. He was a wealthy man who knew blacks almost solely as servants. But, like the ill-fated John Kennedy, he learned quite a bit about them shortly after election.

Roosevelt received black visitors in the White House and he had a number of black men to whom he turned for advice from the very beginning. Robert L. Vann of the *Pittsburgh Courier*, Julian Rainey of Boston, and F. B. Ransom of Indianapolis

Count Basie got his start with big bands in the 1930s, and still had a leading band in the 1970s.

Ella Fitzgerald first won fame with Chick Webb's band.

Cab Calloway was a famous "scat singer" of the period.

were Democrats who had his ear. Both Roosevelt and his wife, Eleanor, visited black organizations and black institutions. Eleanor Roosevelt was a tremendous asset to the president in winning the support of black people. One of her friends was Mary McLeod Bethune, the black educator who headed Bethune-Cookman College and the National Council of Negro Women. Mrs. Roosevelt defied her Washington social critics by inviting the National Council of Negro Women to the White House.

President Roosevelt appointed so many black men to responsible positions in his administration that they became known as his Black Cabinet. While most of the black appointees had positions directly connected with the welfare of black people, some worked in areas of importance to the populace as a whole. William H. Hastie, Eugene Kinkle Jones, Robert C. Weaver, Robert L. Vann, Lawrence A. Oxley, Mrs. Bethune, Frank S. Horne, Edgar Brown, and William J. Trent were some of the more prominent blacks who were a part of Roosevelt's black "brain trust."

Roosevelt's programs to bring the country out of the Depression were quite radical for that period. Under the National Industrial Recovery Act, which was designed to stimulate industry, workers were guaranteed a minimum wage, a forty-hour work week, and the employment of children under sixteen was abolished.

The government's Agricultural Administration Act was designed to help small as well as large farmers in crop reduction programs, but the administration of the program in the South was at some times so crooked and at most times so confused that poor whites as well as poor blacks benefited little from it. One of the biggest gains for the poor to come out of the AAA

Earl "Father" Hines had a solid band through the swing era, adopted a modern approach in the 1940s. Billie Holiday and Lester "Prez" Young (below) were avant-garde musicians of the day.

Marian Anderson sang for thousands at the Lincoln Memorial on Easter Sunday in 1939 after being barred from Constitution Hall by the Daughters of the American Revolution. Richard B. Harrison gave a moving performance as De Lawd in *The Green Pastures*.

was the organization of the Southern Tenant Farmers' Union which became a great aid to poor farmers, both black and white, in the South.

The Farm Security Administration under the liberal Will W. Alexander specifically outlawed discrimination and did much to help black farmers purchase land.

Two programs aimed at youth, the National Youth Administration and the Civilian Conservation Corps, were of great importance to black people. The NYA hired Mrs. Bethune to head the Division of Negro Affairs, and black state and local directors were hired to ensure fair treatment for young blacks in cities and regions where there was a large black population. In the out-of-school program where youths were taught trades that might be beneficial in a war emergency, some 13 percent of the students were black. In this program, sixty-four thousand blacks were able to earn money to help them stay in school.

Segregated Civilian Conservation Corps camps were set up in the state and federal forest lands where teenage youths could work in reforestation and conservation for room, board, clothing, and a small salary. The camps hired educational directors and teachers. Some 200,000 young black men had spent some time in CCC camps before the program ended in 1942.

The Home Owners Loan Corporation and the Federal Housing Authority benefited those attempting to buy homes, and ghetto dwellers were helped through the construction of low-cost housing projects.

The Public Works Administration provided government funds for states to build schools and roads and libraries and hospitals, and the Work Progress Administration provided jobs for those who could work and relief for those who could not. Under the WPA, a man could work in the field for which he had been trained and it was not unusual for an artist to draw his WPA money for painting a mural on a school wall or for teaching children how to sketch and paint. Musicians were paid for playing in community bands, and writers were hired to write local or state histories.

Social Security, one of the most daring

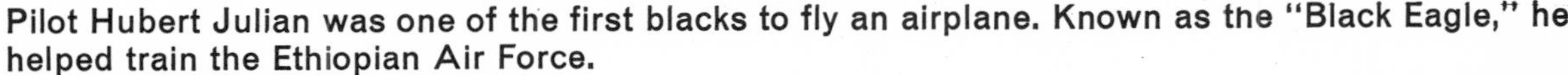

Pilot Hubert Julian was one of the first blacks to fly an airplane. Known as the "Black Eagle," he helped train the Ethiopian Air Force.

of Roosevelt's programs, was established in 1935. It provided old age and unemployment insurance but it was set up so as to exclude many blacks. Agricultural and domestic workers were not covered. This meant that thousands of black farmers in the South, and thousands of black domestic workers all over the country could not participate. The Wages and Hours bill established a minimum wage of 25 cents an hour in 1938, but the bill discriminated against blacks by excluding agricultural and domestic workers.

The measures adopted by Roosevelt got many of the unemployed youth off the street, fed the hungry, housed the poor, and gave men a chance to earn "relief" through labor. Factories began to hum again in the early forties. By this time, Adolf Hitler was spouting his Nazi doctrine of Aryan superiority. And before the decade ended, Europe was again at war. In a little while the United States was a part of World War II.

Despite the Depression, black folk in Harlem enjoyed events like this Elks parade on August 22, 1939.

7

World War II

THE MOOD OF THE BLACK MAN of the early forties was bitter and brooding. He had fought bravely for America in World War I only to return home to find that the democracy he had defended did not exist for him. He had thought of going back to Africa with Garvey, he had joined in A. Philip Randolph's fight for the black man's rights in labor, and he had lived through an impressive black cultural renaissance that had given him a new sense of identity.

Moreover, he had been severely victimized by the Depression of the thirties, and he had suffered an increase in lynchings, beatings, jailings, and other forms of violence. Both North and South America were still largely segregated and economically the black man defined himself as the "last hired, first fired." It was not surprising, then, that when war efforts were stepped up in the early forties, blacks broke into protest at all levels. The black press played a significant role in the pro-

tests. The *Atlanta Daily World*, the Norfolk *Journal and Guide*, the *Pittsburgh Courier* and the *Chicago Defender* were unrelenting in their exposure and commentary on racial inequities in America and abroad. They sent war correspondents to the European and Pacific theaters and ran big headlines on discrimination and segregation in the armed forces. Sweden's Gunnar Myrdal said perceptively of the black press of this period:

Again the inconsistency between expressed war aims and domestic policy becomes glaring. Again there is discrimination in the Army, Navy and Air Force, and in the war industries. Again there are Negro heroes, unrecognized by the whites, to praise. And again the low morale of the Negro people becomes a worry to the government. Again white leaders come out with declarations that justice must be given to Negroes. The administration makes cautious concessions. Negro leaders are more determined. All this makes good copy.

The *Afro-American* and the *Courier* became searingly critical of discrimination in war plants and army camps and the *Courier* initiated a highly successful "Double V" campaign—for victory at home and victory abroad. The War Department, having become more aware of the power of the black press, kept its top executives informed with a weekly "Report of Trends in the Colored Press." Black newspaper, journal, and magazine editors like Carl Murphy, P. B. Young, Adam Clayton Powell Jr., and C. A. Scott were more wary and less "trustful of high sounding slogans and bounteous promises." While still striving to keep their readers loyal to America and to the cause for which they were fighting, the black editors encouraged blacks to improve their status while the war was going on, rather than wait patiently, as they had done in World War I, until it was over. The increased militancy of the black press so stirred public sentiment, in fact, that the government briefly considered prosecuting black publishers for impeding the war effort. Under pressure, however, the government reconsidered this move.

Dorie Miller saved the life of his ship's captain and shot down four enemy planes at Pearl Harbor, for which act of heroism he received the Navy Cross from Admiral Chester W. Nimitz on May 27, 1942. He was later killed in combat.

Dr. Charles Drew, chief surgeon at Freedmen's Hospital in Washington D.C., developed techniques for extracting blood plasma, and established a blood bank and collection service which saved many lives during the war.

During the two years prior to Pearl Harbor, the black man faced two serious problems. One was that he was barred from participating in the enormous national defense industries. The labor situation had changed and defense work needed skilled workers.

In the fall of 1940, the federal government made provision for training people who sought defense employment, saying there would be "no discrimination on account of race, creed or color." The government provided that where separate schools were required by law for separate population groups, equal provisions would be made for the facilities and training of like quality. Because employment opportunities had been so slow in materializing, blacks hesitated to enter the training schools. With the rapid move of white skilled workers into the well-paying jobs, there were plenty of openings in the nondefense, unskilled and service capacities —jobs that blacks could get with a minimum of training. But these positions did not absorb many unemployed blacks, or provide an opportunity for getting into the mainstream of the defense industry.

Despite the need for and the availability of black skilled workers, discrimination continued. The president of North American Aviation said: "Regardless of their trainings as aircraft workers, we will not employ Negroes in the North American plant. It is against company policy." This attitude was prevalent in hundreds of defense plants across the country.

The second major problem that the black man faced was discrimination in the armed forces. The Congress of 1866 had provided that "the enlisted men of two regiments of Infantry and . . . the enlisted men of two regiments of Cavalry shall be colored men." In keeping with this legislation, the Twenty-fourth and Twenty-fifth infantry regiments and the Ninth and Tenth cavalry regiments, all with an impressive history of combat, had been maintained in the regular army after World War I. In 1939, two black quarter-

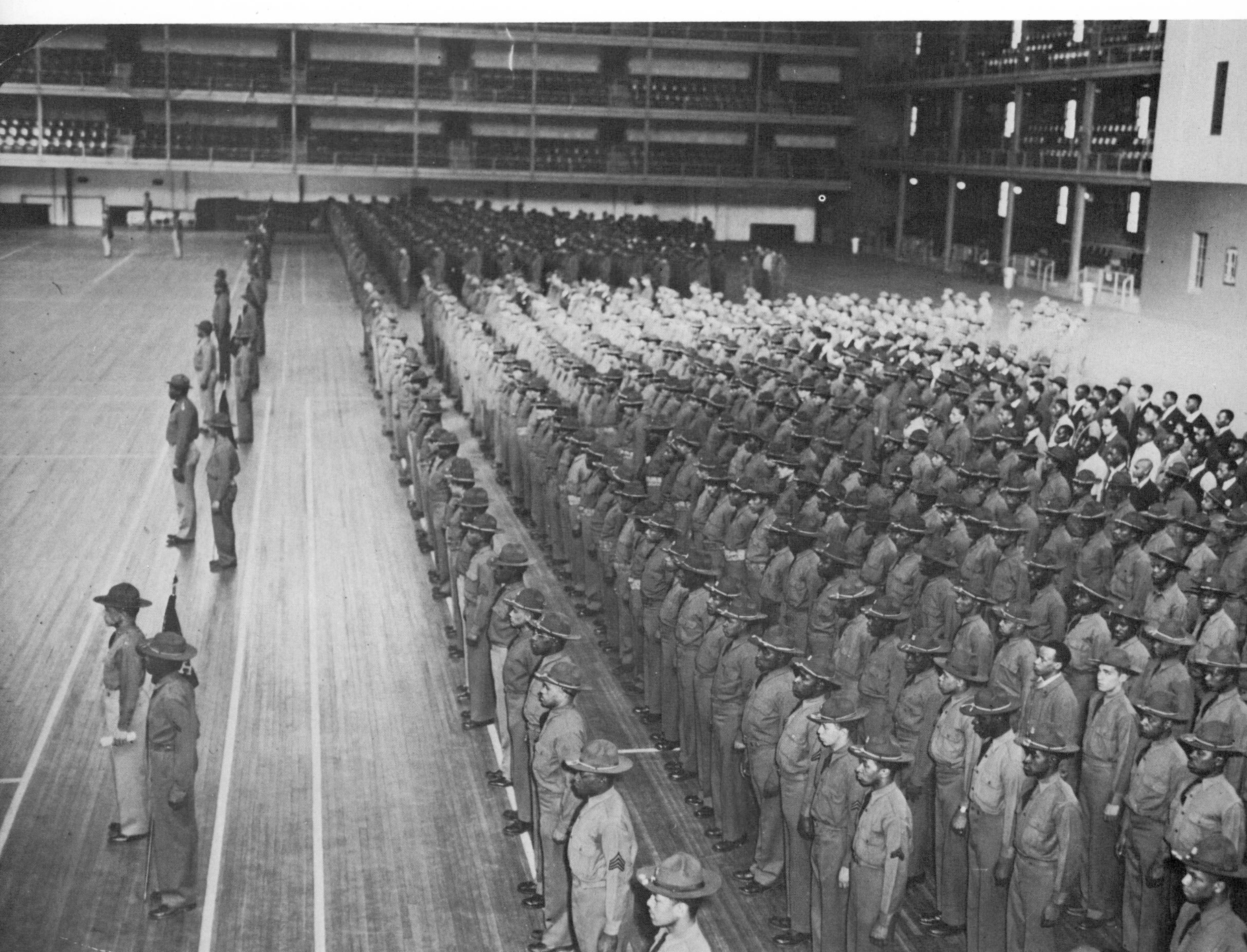

An all-black peacetime National Guard unit, the 369th, was mustered into the regular army in Harlem in January, 1941.

master regiments—the Twenty-fourth and the Forty-eighth—were partially organized as truck companies, and soon after the 249th Field Artillery Regiment was activated. The Seventy-sixth and the Seventy-seventh, two coast artillery units, which would later be expanded into regiments, became the first black units in this type of combat service. The Forty-first Engineer Regiment and additional truck companies, including elements of the Thirty-first Quartermaster Regiment were also organized. A single chemical warfare company was also added.

In the National Guard there were the 369th, 184th and 372nd regiments. Early in the expansion program, the 369th was converted into the 369th Coast Artillery, and the 184th into the 184th Field Artillery. Despite this expansion of black troops, the regular army of 230,000 contained only 4,450 blacks. Most of these troops were in the army and totally segregated from white troops in housing, training, and combat. The announced War Department policy was restructured to keep down the level of black enlistments. The navy and the Air Force staunchly refused blacks, except as messmen and ground workers, and kept the number of black enlistees at an appallingly low minimum.

To add insult to injury, the American Red Cross announced in November, 1941, that it would not accept the blood of black donors for blood banks for wounded soldiers. This decision was made, they said, after the army and navy received complaints from white Southerners who refused transfusions with "Negro blood." The Red Cross kept separate blood banks for blacks and whites until Dr. Charles Drew, a black physician, and chief surgeon at Freedman's Hospital in Washington, D.C., took leave to work on blood plasma techniques. At Columbia University Medical School in New York City, he found a way to preserve the plasma in

The Twenty-fifth Regiment, one of the oldest black units in the army, was reactivated in the early years of the war.

blood banks for emergency use. Drew's brilliant collection service for both the United States and Great Britain ultimately saved the lives of many soldiers and civilians.

Another irony of World War II occurred during the attack on Pearl Harbor. When the Japanese launched their historic attack on December 7, 1941, there was a black mess attendant, Dorie Miller, aboard the warship *Arizona*. In the heat of the battle, Miller dragged his wounded captain to safety, manned a machine gun, and downed four enemy planes. Miller was awarded the Navy Cross a year later. His actions at Pearl Harbor were described as "the only American victory on that day."

These events and the War Department's discriminatory policies against blacks in industry and the armed services caused a great deal of black unrest and protest. A. Philip Randolph, head of the powerful Brotherhood of Sleeping Car Porters, proposed a July, 1941, March on Washington to demand an executive order that would ban discrimination in war industries and apprenticeship programs.

A platoon of black marine recruits presents arms.

The nation's first black general, Benjamin O. Davis Sr., flanked by Truman K. Gibson Jr., black civilian aide to the secretary of war, and his son, Colonel Benjamin O. Davis Jr. He examines a quartermaster company punishment book (below) and inspects a signal corps crew in France (r.).

"Nothing stirs and shapes public sentiment like physical action," Randolph said at the time, and emphasized that unless black demands were met one hundred thousand blacks would stage a nonviolent March on Washington.

President Franklin D. Roosevelt opposed the march, as did most whites and some blacks. Randolph was called to New York City Hall by Mrs. Roosevelt and Fiorello LaGuardia, who tried to dissuade him. Randolph would not budge. President Roosevelt later sent for Randolph and Walter White of the NAACP and T.

U.S.
U.S.

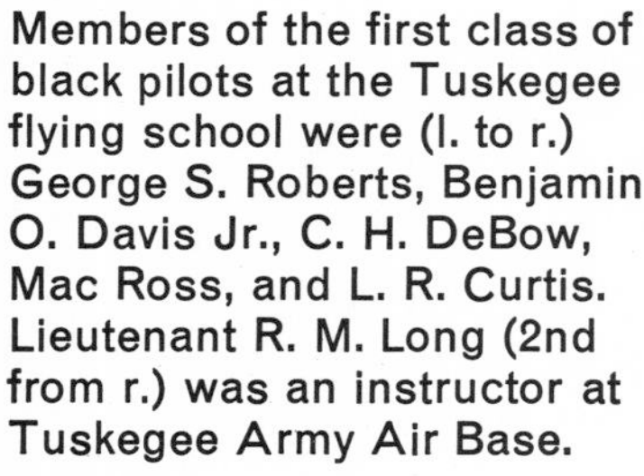

Members of the first class of black pilots at the Tuskegee flying school were (l. to r.) George S. Roberts, Benjamin O. Davis Jr., C. H. DeBow, Mac Ross, and L. R. Curtis. Lieutenant R. M. Long (2nd from r.) was an instructor at Tuskegee Army Air Base.

Arnold Hill, acting executive of the National Urban League. The president challenged Randolph's right to put pressure on the White House and said the government was doing all it could and intended to do more to end discrimination at home and abroad. Again neither Randolph nor his colleagues would budge and a rather heated discussion ensued. Randolph insisted that he would have an executive order banning discrimination or he would have his march. Seven days later President Roosevelt issued Executive Order 8802 which banned discrimination in war industries and apprenticeship programs. The order said in part:

> . . . It is the duty of employers and labor organizations to provide for the full and equitable participation of all workers in the defense industries without discrimination. . . . All departments and agencies of the Government of the United States concerned with vocational and training programs for defense production shall take special measures appropriate to assure that such programs are administered without discrimination. . . . All contracting agencies of the Government of the United States shall include in all defense contracts hereafter negotiated by them a provision obligating the contractor not to discriminate against any worker. . . .

The president also named an FEP Committee that included two blacks, Earl B. Dickerson, a Chicago lawyer, and Milton P. Webster, vice-president of the Brotherhood of Sleeping Car Porters. This document read in part:

> There is established in the Office of Production

Management a Committee on Fair Employment Practices, which shall consist of a chairman and four other members to be appointed by the President.

On the day of the issuance of the order —June 25, 1941—Randolph called off the March on Washington. But the executive order did not solve the problems of racial discrimination which persisted in industry and the armed services.

The Office of Education was unable to implement the provisions of the order. Figures released by this federal agency in January, 1942, showed that in eighteen Southern and Border States, where 22 per-

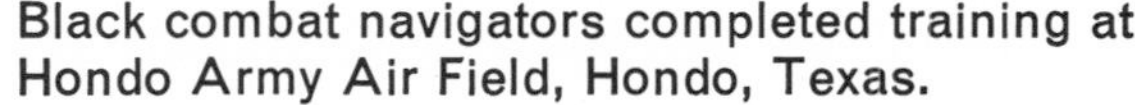

Black combat navigators completed training at Hondo Army Air Field, Hondo, Texas.

Pilots of the 332nd Fighter Group leave their quarters in the Mediterranean Theater (above). A mechanic of the 332nd repairs a Mustang fighter plane (right).

cent of the total population was black, only 3,215 blacks, or 4 percent of the total trainees, were enrolled in pre-employment and refresher training courses. Out of 4,630 training courses in the Southern States, only 194 were open to blacks.

In the midst of this controversy and an approaching presidential election, Roosevelt announced several black appointments. William H. Hastie, dean of the Howard University Law School, was appointed civilian aide to Secretary of War Henry Stimson; Colonel Benjamin O. Davis Sr. was promoted to brigadier general, the nation's first black general; Robert C. Weaver was made director of a defense work program, and Colonel Campbell Johnson, head of reserve officer training at Howard University, was named special aide to draft director Lewis B. Hershey.

IN THE MEANTIME, pressures continued to build against the government. Black and white newspapers continued their assault on discrimination in the armed forces and national defense, and periodicals began to carry editorials discouraging blacks from entering the service.

The army was the only branch which accepted blacks routinely. The Air Force had a few blacks in construction companies. The navy only took blacks as messmen. In all branches, blacks had separate quarters, training facilities, and entertainment.

The public pressure prompted the signing of the Selective Service Act on September 14, 1940, which contained a clause

Members of the 332nd listen to flight instructions. Colonel Davis (left) was commander of the group.

barring racial discrimination. It also contained a quota clause for the induction of blacks. The drafters of the bill had been influenced by a Committee on Participation of Negroes in the War, set up by the *Pittsburgh Courier*. To the bitter disappointment of its drafters and supporters, subsequent reinterpretation of the bill by army officials rendered it virtually ineffective in ending segregation.

The Air Force proposed that black enlistees be placed in air base detachments to be trained and employed as members of air base groups. The base detachment was intended to prevent mixing of blacks and whites in the same unit. Subsequently, the Air Corps organized nine aviation training squadrons to "take care of the [9 percent] colored selectees allotted to the Air Corps," by the Selective Service Act. These squadrons, whose duties were vaguely defined, were established at every major air base. What would be done with the black airmen was left to the discretion of each base commander. It certainly was not the intent of the Air Corps at this point to train blacks as pilots.

The formation of these squadrons, however, had been prompted by a 1941 NAACP suit against the War Department. The NAACP suit was filed by Yancey Williams, a Howard University student who filed suit against Secretary of War Stimson and other government officials who refused to consider his application for enlistment in the Air Corps as a flying cadet. Howard University was, at the time, the site of intensive short courses providing engineering defense training under the U.S. Office of Education. The Air Corps had long been an attraction for bright young men, both black and white, because of the challenge it offered. But qualified blacks had been consistently refused flight training.

A short time after Williams's suit, the War Department announced the formation of the first black Air Corps squadron to be located near Tuskegee Institute in Alabama, in cooperation with the school. There were many objections to the formation of an all-black air base.

Officers of the 99th, including Lieutenant Colonel George S. Roberts (far right), who succeeded Davis as commander.

The black airmen's school was dedicated on July 19, 1941. This marked the formal beginning of the 99th Pursuit Squadron. The base, which was at first totally unsuitable for training pilots, was converted into an airport by Hilyard Robinson and McKissack and McKissack, black architects and contractors. Under pressure the War Department appropriated nearly two million dollars for the conversion.

On August 25, 1941, the first class of thirteen black cadets began primary training at the 66th Army Air Forces Flying Training Detachment, instructed by civilian pilots, with supervision and administrative work handled by army personnel. Moton Field, named for Dr. Robert Russa Moton, second president of

A black platoon in search of a German sniper surrounds a French farm house. In Italy black troops of the 370th Regiment advance across the Arno River against German positions.

Pinned down by sniper fire, members of the 365th Regiment participate in allied action in Italy.

Tuskegee Institute, was built in 1941 for Army Primary Training, as a facility of the Institute's Division of Aeronautics.

The training schedule of cadets called for five weeks of pre-flight training followed by thirty weeks of primary, basic, and advanced training. By March, 1942, five of the first cadets received their wings. One of the first graduates was Benjamin O. Davis Jr., who would later, as Colonel Davis, lead the black pilots to honor and acclaim. Davis was a West Point Military Academy graduate and had been serving as an aide to his father, Brigadier General Davis, at Fort Riley, Kansas.

The first squadron was formed in October, 1942, and in April, 1943, was sent to French Morocco for a month's intensive training under experienced combat fliers. Their record after that was one of combat triumph. A subsequent War Department release said:

> [The Ninety-ninth] flew its first mission over an air base at Fardjouna. . . . Other early missions were over the island of Pantelleria, Italian stronghold guarding the Sicilian straits. Six of its

pilots had their first brush with enemy aircraft over Pantelleria, and pilots of the Ninety-ninth dive-bombed Pantelleria daily until it surrendered on June 11, 1943. . . . By the middle of July, the Ninety-ninth was escorting bombers over Italy. In a dogfight over Sciacca, Italy, one day, First Lieutenant Charles B. Hall, of Brazil, Indiana, shot down the first Axis plane officially credited to the Ninety-ninth Squadron. On that same day, the Ninety-ninth, flying close escort for . . . bombers, probably destroyed two more German planes and damaged three . . . In one of the fiercest air battles of the Italian campaign, over the Anzio beachhead, south of Rome, Negro pilots of the Ninety-ninth Squadron scored eight confirmed victories over the Germans . . . the largest number (of hits) credited to any single squadron that day. . . . In ten days over Anzio beachhead, the Ninety-ninth brought down 16 enemy planes, and received special commendations of ranking Army Air Forces officials.

In a year's time the Ninety-ninth had flown five hundred missions and 3,728 sorties. The squadron had only lost twelve pilots. The War Department commended the squadron and its commander for this low casualty figure.

In the meantime, Colonel Davis had released his command of the Ninety-ninth to Major George S. Roberts, to return to the states to command Tuskegee's 332nd Fighter Group. The 332nd was activated in October, 1942, and trained at Tuskegee and at Selfridge Field, Michigan. In October, 1943, Colonel Davis took charge of the 332nd, and the first class of black navigation pilots began training at Hondo Field, Texas. Blacks were insisting on the training of bombardier pilots and some of the Hondo trainees were sent to New Mexico for bombardier training.

Meanwhile, blacks had been accepted for paratroop training at Fort Benning, Georgia. In February, 1944, a unit designated as the 555th Parachute Infantry Company, became the first black para-

A wounded soldier of the 365th Infantry is carried down an Italian hillside during a Fifth Army battle.

Members of an armored tank division spearhead an attack.

chute unit. The same month, the 332nd Fighter Group became an active part of the Twelfth Air Force in the Mediterranean Theater, where it was later joined by the crack Ninety-ninth. By 1944, the combined 332nd was operating from Italian bases, as part of the Mediterranean Coastal Air Force. The unit flew in convoy protection and harbor patrol missions, and in close support of advancing allied armies, in dive-bombing operations. The 332nd battled more than one hundred enemy fighters near Udine, Italy, downing five. Ultimately, the 332nd destroyed a total of 111 enemy planes and damaged an estimated 69. In one historic battle, the 332nd sank an enemy destroyer with machine gun fire off the Istrian Peninsula. The 332nd received hundreds of group and individual citations.

Tuskegee's thirty-fourth and last graduating class in June, 1946, included nine cadets and brought the total number of fliers trained at the school to 992. Pilot production at Tuskegee reached its peak in March, 1945, when thirty-eight pilots received wings. The TAAF also produced hundreds of technicians and specialists.

In September, 1946, the Tuskegee base was declared surplus by the Air Force and its officers transferred to the Lockbourne Army Air Base in Columbus, Ohio, to join the allblack 477th Composite Group.

THE ACCEPTANCE OF THE BLACK man in the navy took an entirely different turn and resulted not only in his widespread induction, but in integration. In many ways, the developments in the navy were a paradox because the navy had offered the most resistance to black troops. The navy's early policies were ably stated by National Urban League president Lester B. Granger, who served as special adviser to the Secretary of the Navy for a short period in 1945.

> World War II started [he said] with the Navy presenting a dismal record and policy in the use of Negro troops and personnel. Until the attack on Pearl Harbor, and for several months thereafter, Negroes were accepted in the Navy only in the Steward's branch . . . . This branch was composed of men who served the personal needs of commis-

An all-black crew operates an M-8 armored car in combat training in the European Theater.

sioned officers in their living and eating. The policy had been inherited by our wartime Navy leadership. It was established during the administration of President Woodrow Wilson shortly after the close of World War I. This discriminatory policy temporarily closed a long chapter of naval history written by Negroes in naval service from the days of Commander Perry on Lake Champlain down to the close of World War I. The shift of policy was announced boldly by closing down all Negro naval enlistments and reopening them several months later only for service as steward's mates. . . . Navy Secretary Frank Knox held stubbornly to this policy even after the outbreak of World War II. Presumably backed by his ranking advisers, the Secretary insisted, in the face of strong protest, that the morale of the service would be disrupted if this racial policy were changed. Here was the "old regular Navy," so far as Negro service was concerned.

In the four years after Pearl Harbor, blacks by the tens of thousands, both men and women, had sought induction into the navy. Many of them received assignment in a variety of service duties. Near the end of the war, the navy, unlike the other military branches, was accepting black enlistments without discrimination.

Early in 1942, reluctant naval authorities announced that blacks would be accepted for general service. A number of

Light tank crews stand by for orders to clean out Nazi machine-gun nests in Coburg, Germany.

blacks enlisted immediately, but the criticism did not disappear as blacks noted that general service, as defined by Secretary Knox, meant only that a large number of blacks were performing the dangerous and unglamorous work of handling munitions and loading ships. Dramatic evidence of the black disenchantment with the "new" navy was seen in three mass demonstrations: a mutiny, a race riot, and a hunger strike.

The mass mutiny occurred at Mare Island, California, following a mammoth ammunitions explosion at nearby Port Chicago Ammunition Depot. More than two hundred blacks were killed. Practically the entire personnel was black. A few days later when 250 blacks were assigned to load an ammunition ship at Mare Island, they refused to work, claiming inadequate training and safety provisions. Faced with punitive action, two hundred returned to work, but fifty resisted. They were court-martialed for mutiny and sentenced to from eight to fifteen years at hard labor, plus dishonorable discharge. The efforts of Attorney Thurgood Marshall, who appeared in their behalf, resulted in their sentences being suspended.

In the Pacific, on Guam Island, an even more serious disturbance occurred when arguments and fights between black and white seamen resulted in a Christmas season race riot. After a black sailor was killed by a white serviceman, a group of

Awarded the Bronze Star for his heroism, Sergeant Walter King receives congratulations in Germany from Major General Hugh J. Gaffey.

blacks broke into the barracks armory, seized weapons and trucks, and headed for the Marine Guard barracks. The blacks were intercepted en route, arrested at machine gun point and court-martialed. They were charged with illegal possession of government property and incitement to riot. They were found guilty and sentenced to from five to twenty years. Walter White of the NAACP came to their defense and state-

A black military police unit poses for photographs at their Columbus, Georgia, base.

side organizations began work on their behalf. Early in January, 1946, it was announced by the Navy Department that the thirty-six men remaining in confinement would be released and cleared.

A two-day hunger strike by a black navy construction battalion was staged at Camp Rousseau, Port Hueneme, California in March, 1945, in mass protest against Jim Crow practices and the lack of promotions. It was a peaceful demonstration. After the first day, the station commandant ordered the sailors to the chow hall. The men went but still refused to eat. The battalion of black Seabees had been overseas for months and, after meritorious service, had been returned for rest and reassignment. They charged unfair and racially discriminatory treatment by the white officer in command. When news

Men of the Fourth Cavalry Brigade leave the West Riding Hall at Fort Riley, Kansas.

of the strike hit the front pages of the black press, hundreds of organizations interceded in behalf of the strikers.

Before the strike, the navy had denied that the accused commander, Mississippian P. J. McBean, had discriminated against the seamen. The commander was relieved of his command and after a period of rest the black Seabees were returned to active duty overseas. On April 5, 1945, it was announced by the War Department that the discharges of fourteen of the fifteen punished Seabees were being changed from "undesirable" to "discharged under honorable conditions."

These incidents and attendant pressures served to speed up steps already underway to remove the worst aspects of segregation and discrimination in the navy. The Bureau of Naval Personnel had

A road-building crew of engineer troops participates in a New Guinea offensive.

initiated increased assignment of blacks to advanced training schools and to ratings as petty officers. The navy had also established special officers' classes and had commissioned a dozen black officers. Assignments of blacks to service on auxiliary and shore patrol crafts were made, and reduction of the large proportions of blacks in supply bases and ammunition depots was effected. In addition, black machinists and other technicians were assigned to naval air stations, ship repair establishments, and navy offices.

As the result of a special study by the Fahy Committee, indoctrination courses were established for white officers in command of black seamen, and efforts were made to weed out white officers who were emotionally and psychologically unsuited for association with black troops.

An important influence in the change of the navy was the new secretary of navy, James Forrestal, who took office after Secretary Knox. Reacting to continued clamor and protest—heightened by the riot and strikes—Forrestal immediately implemented the navy's

An engineer unit lines up for food in Assam, India, where the unit helped in the construction of a connection to the old Burma Road.

planned program and initiated new ones aimed at invalidating any charge that the navy was discriminating against its black seamen. Forrestal conferred in December, 1944, with a group of black newspaper publishers and, early in the spring of 1945, he appointed Lester Granger as a civilian aide to counsel him on a program that called for the acceptance of enlisted blacks in the regular navy, marines and Coast Guard. He announced that black reserve officers would be allowed to apply for regular navy commissions. Blacks could serve on all combat ships and the proportion of black personnel on any vessel or activity was reduced to make segregated accommodation impracticable.

Blacks in service on auxiliary and combat vessels increased steadily. At war's end, such ships were staffed with a 10 percent quota of blacks in both Atlantic and Pacific operations. The number of commissioned black officers increased significantly. At naval training schools, like the Great Lakes (Ill.) Naval Training Station, blacks and whites studied and worked together, and hundreds of black petty and commissioned officers commanded racially mixed units. Blacks served in every technical service of the navy, including aviation machinists and radar, and increasing numbers of blacks were placed in other naval services like the Seabees, the marines, the Coast Guard and the merchant marines.

Although there were innovative programs in both the Air Corps and the naval services, the army continued to segregate blacks throughout the war. Most of the army bases were located in the South (where climate and economy facilitated training), and there were many racial incidents.

In the fall of 1940, the War Department issued a directive that "the strength of the Negro personnel of the Army of the United States will be maintained on the general basis of proportion of the Negro population of the country," and that "Negro organizations will be established in

In England, Major Charity B. Adams and aide Captain Abbie N. Campbell inspect WACS assigned to overseas duty. Pfc. Johnnie Mae Welton conducts a serology experiment at the Fort Jackson Station Hospital in Fort Jackson, South Carolina.

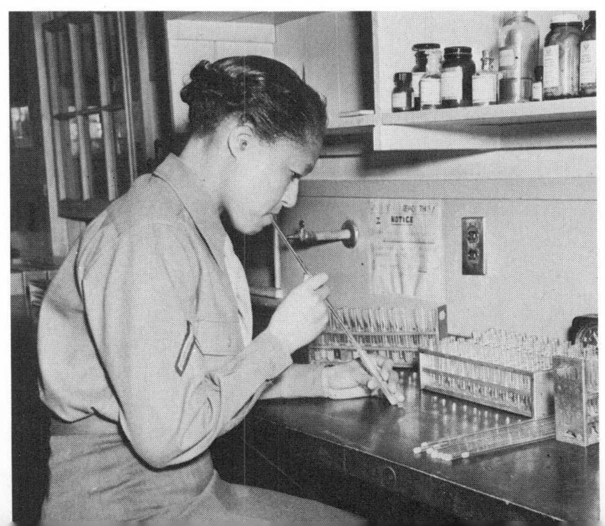

each major branch of the service, combatant as well as non-combatant." As a result of this directive, there was an expansion of previously existing black units and the creation of additional organizations. Early in 1942, the Secretary of War announced a significant recruitment of additional black soldiers for new types of services, such as task destroyer units and some Interior Military Police battalions.

The officer personnel of the peacetime regular army was very small. After the inauguration of the Selective Service System, the army began to utilize the five hundred black officers of the National Guard and reserve. At the end of 1941, the problem of black officers in the army, just as in other branches, had mostly to do

Members of the first destroyer manned predominantly by blacks, stand before the USS *Mason* at the Boston Navy Yard.

with training. An earlier statement from the War Department had established that policy on training of officers would extend to black and white alike. "When officer candidate schools are established, opportunity will be given to Negroes to qualify for reserve commissions." After much deliberation it was decided that black and white officer candidates would be trained in the same schools and classes. This decision became the basic policy of the War Department, except for the Air Corps.

Despite appearances, it soon became apparent that there was still racial discrimination in officer candidate selection. In the first half year of the new candidate training, fewer than thirty black soldiers were admitted to the schools, although the black enlistees had increased significantly.

In another area, the Southern location of a majority of army camps was detrimental to the black soldiers' morale. Segregation and discrimination prevailed both within the camps and in the surrounding communities. Some black soldiers were murdered. Many were assaulted and humiliated by whites. In addition, there was the problem of the white military policemen. The army did not authorize the training and use of black policemen until hundreds of black soldiers had been assaulted by white MP's. The utilization of black MP's was never effective. Some were not armed; others carried pistols with no bullets; and still others could only arrest blacks.

While touring army camps in 1941, *Pittsburgh Courier* editor P. L. Prattis commented: "The Negro area, in nine cases out of ten, was in the most inaccessible section of the camp. . . . At Camp Lee, Negro soldiers told the writer that they had started at the center of the camp and had successively cleared up areas which were turned over to future incoming white troops while the Negroes were always kept in the woods." Prattis visited other camps and observed that the quarters for blacks were inferior and often isolated from the main camp. All of these conditions unquestionably lowered the black soldier's morale and effectiveness.

Captain Hugh Mulzac (l.), of the *Booker T. Washington*, was the first black commander in the merchant marines.

After touring army camps both North and South, Brigadier General Benjamin O. Davis Sr., said in a 1943 memorandum:

[The morale of Northern soldiers was] very

Nine black sailors were commissioned from the ranks by the U.S. Navy in 1944.

Demonstrators in front of the White House in 1946 petitioned President Truman to declare martial law in a Monroe, Georgia, racial disturbance.

much different from those of the colored officers and soldiers at the stations in the Southern States . . . . there is still great dissatisfaction on the part of the colored people and the soldiers. They feel that, regardless of how much they strive to meet War Department requirements, there is no change in the attitude of the War Department. The colored officers and soldiers feel that they are denied the protection and awards that ordinarily result from good behavior and proper performance of duty. . . . The colored man in uniform receives nothing but hostility from community officials . . . . The colored man in uniform is expected by the War Department to develop a high morale in a community that offers him nothing but humiliation and mistreatment. . . . Officers of the War Department General Staff have refused to attempt any remedial action to eliminate Jim Crow. In fact, the Army, by its directions and by actions of commanding officers, has introduced Jim Crow practices in areas, both at home and abroad, where they have not hitherto been practiced. . . .

An unfortunate incident surrounding the efficiency of the allblack Ninety-second Division contributed to the low morale of black soldiers and created a nationwide furor. The Ninety-second was conspicuous for its part in the Mediterranean Theater of Operations. At the time of its departure from Fort Huachuca, Arizona, in June, 1944, it was composed of the 365th, 370th and 371st Infantry regiments and the 597th, 598th, 599th and 600th Field Artillery battalions. A few months later, it was joined by the 366th Infantry. In Italy the Ninety-second served with the Fifth Army.

In its first major offensive, the Ninety-second crossed the Arno River, capturing the city of Lucca in September, 1944. Later in the same year, after capturing several towns and considerable territory from the Germans, the Ninety-second withdrew in the face of a surprise attack by the enemy. The soldiers were able to resume their position within a few days, and recaptured all lost ground. In early 1945, an offensive of the Ninety-second in the area of the Cinqualle Canal, became the major object of unfavorable criticism. After four days of fighting and the capture of some territory, the Ninety-second withdrew with severe losses in men and equipment. A misinterpreted description of the occurrence by Truman K. Gibson, black civilian aide to the Secretary of War, created a national controversy. Gibson made a tour of the Ninety-second Division sector in Italy and spoke of "a melting away" and "more or less panicky retreats."

The emphasis in the Gibson report, however, was not on the "panicky retreats" but on certain abnormal conditions which could easily result in less than normal performance. But his statements had been taken out of context and it was not until after considerable investigation and special reports on the Ninety-second that the controversy was cleared up and the contents of the report taken in their entirety. The division was later commended.

By the end of the war, members of the division had earned more than twelve thousand citations.

A bleeding man is arrested by police during the Harlem riots of 1943.

Because of need and protests, the number of blacks in the armed services rose sharply between 1940 and 1945. At the end of 1941, there were more than one hundred thousand blacks in the armed services, with a large percentage of this total being unassigned or in miscellaneous detachments. After Pearl Harbor, the number of black enlisted men increased to two hundred thousand.

In 1942, army totals reached 450,000 blacks with 90,000 of these being on overseas duty. By 1943 the army reported 582,000 blacks in service with significant increases in the ranks of the cavalry, engineering, commissioned officers, and medics. The navy totals increased from 4,000 in 1940 to 74,000 in 1942.

In the Coast Guard there were three thousand blacks by 1943. Fifty percent of these black guardsmen were apprentice seamen and 50 percent were mess attendants. By March, 1944, there were 968 black officers and petty officers in the Coast Guard and black enlisted men numbered four thousand.

There were 8,500 blacks in the Marine Corps. There were no black commissioned officers in the corps in 1943. The first black commissioned officer in the Marine Corps was not appointed until November, 1945.

Among the first black women admitted

Bishop Edwin Collins speaks from a balcony to calm rioting crowds in Harlem.

Motorcycle patrols and black soldiers patrol Harlem streets.

to the WAVES in November, 1944, were Harriet Ida Pickens and Francis Eliza Wills, who became officer candidates and were graduated in December, 1944. The number of black women in the WAVES never rose to more than sixty or seventy in a total of eight thousand.

By 1946, there were well over a hundred black nurses in the army and more than three thousand black women, including 115 officers, in the Women's Army Corps (WACS).

By the middle of 1942, blacks were graduating from the three-month officer

Army troops arrive in Harlem for riot duty.

Army troops restore order after the 1943 Detroit riots, in which twenty-nine were killed.

candidate courses at the rate of nearly two hundred monthly. The total number of black officers on duty at the end of 1942 was approximately two thousand, a significant increase.

By the end of the war more than 7,500 blacks had become officers, including Brigadier General Davis, thirty-four colonels and lieutenant colonels. In 1945 the number of black naval officers rose to sixty.

As the war plot thickened, blacks began to go to the front lines in ever increasing numbers. Slightly under 9 percent of the 259,173 black troops in the European Theater of Operations one week after VE-Day, in 1945, belonged to combat organizations.

Twenty-two black combat units participated in the American Expeditionary Forces campaign against the Wehrmacht. The 320th Barrage Balloon Battalion was the only black combat unit to take part in the initial landings on the Normandy coast on June 6, 1945. Classified as an antiaircraft unit, it was the only American

DAVE'S
CORNER
DAVE'S CUT RATE DRUG
ISIT DAVE'S
PRESCRIPTION

Two black congressmen during the war years: William Dawson (D., Ill., standing) and Adam Clayton Powell, Jr. (D., N.Y.). Judge William Hastie (left), a government aide during the war who resigned his post because of bias, addresses people of Virgin Islands as their new governor.

unit of its type in Europe. Men from the 320th waded ashore in the early hours of D-Day, struggling with their "flying beer bottles," dug in with infantrymen of the First and Twenty-ninth, and, under fierce enemy fire, erected a protective curtain of silver barrage balloons that were highly effective in combating German aircraft. Black artillerymen of the 333rd Field Artillery Battalion landed with 155-millimeter howitzers in Normandy on D-Day plus 10 and performed their first mission with the Eighth Army Corps, which was to fire in support of the Ninetieth Infantry Division and take part in the bloody hill battles at St. Jores, Lessay, and Forêt de Monte Castret.

The 333rd also swept through Avranches into Brittany and battled a German counteroffensive in Belgium and across the German border. With several other U.S. units, the 333rd faced the deadly attack of Karl von Rundstedt and the loss in men and equipment was severe.

Mourners at the funeral procession of President Roosevelt on April 14, 1945.

Survivors of this battle and liberated prisoners later told of the stubborn resistance and high courage of the 333rd, even after large groups of men had been surrounded by the enemy.

The 969th Field Artillery Battalion, the only black artillery unit in Europe to receive a Presidential Unit Citation, fought through campaigns in Normandy and northern France, providing artillery backing for a number of U.S. divisions. When the Ardennes break-through occurred, the 969th received orders to displace its guns and withdraw in the direction of Bastogne, Belgium. On reaching Bastogne, the 969th became involved in the famed Battle of Bastogne and earned a place in American military history as one of the units of the gallant garrison that fought against overwhelming odds to save the strategically vital rail and road junction. The 969th won a special citation for this battle.

The 777th Field Artillery Battalion was the only black 4.5-inch gun unit in the European Theater and fought with the Ninth Army. The 777th fired the first American artillery round across the Rhine River near München-Gladbach. Other ETO black artillery units were the 999th Field Artillery Battalion which fired its 8-inch howitzers from lower Normandy to central Germany and the 578th that helped to stem the Nazi tide in the Ardennes.

The 761st Tank Battalion, as attached armor of the 26th Infantry in the Third Army, was the first black tank unit to go into action. The 761st fought in six European countries—France, Holland, Belgium, Luxembourg, Germany, and Austria—and at various times was attached to the Third, Seventh, and Ninth armies. During the European campaigns the bat-

President Truman met with black leaders to discuss racial inequities in the armed services.

Actor Paul Robeson, a militant activist during the war years, shown here as Othello. Richard Wright's novel, *Native Son,* was published in 1941. Black poetess Gwendolyn Brooks and son Henry Blakely Jr. share the news of the 1950 Pulitzer Prize award for her book, *Annie Allen.*

talion furnished tank support for several infantry divisions and the Seventeenth Airborne during the Battle of the Bulge. These black tankers also spearheaded the famous Task Force Rhine which crashed through the rugged mountain defenses of the Siegfried Line. The Task Force Rhine also included another black outfit, the 614th Tank Destroyer Battalion.

The 784th Tank Unit assisted in the crossing of both the Roer and Rhine rivers. In the fighting that followed these crossings, the 614th was attached to the

Black inroads in the movie industry were made in this 1943 production of *Stormy Weather*, featuring Bill (Bojangles) Robinson and Lena Horne.

Todd Duncan (center) and Anne Brown (right) played leading roles in *Porgy and Bess*.

Seventh Army. The 614th was cited for heroic performance of duty in France, where it remained with the Seventh Army until the end of the war.

In December, 1944, black troops answered a call for additional troops in the European Theater. Some 2,500 black volunteers were trained at a ground forces reinforcement command depot at Noyons, France, and were later committed to action with infantry and armored divisions of the First and Seventh armies.

During the campaign against the German army, 5,500 black Signal Corps troops earned laurels for laying communications wire from the hedgerowed fields of Normandy, across France, Luxembourg, and Belgium, deep into Germany. In chemical warfare, one of the greatest artificial fogs in military history was created in December, 1944, by the

Another World War II film was *Tales of Manhattan* with (l.-r.) Ethel Waters, Eddie (Rochester) Anderson, and Miss Horne.

allblack 161st Smoke Generator Company when it shrouded the upper Saar River Valley with a dense cloud of fog that completely obscured the movements of one entire division. Other black chemical warfare units were the Twenty-fifth, the Thirty-second and Thirty-fourth. More than 2,442 blacks served in chemical warfare.

Blacks also participated in front-line divisions which handled ammunition, road building, medicine, engineering, transport trucking, and amphibian details.

In the Pacific Theater, black soldiers distinguished themselves on every front. The Ninety-sixth Engineer Battalion—later the Ninety-sixth Engineer Regiment—landed in Port Moresby, New Guinea, in 1942 as the first American troops in New Guinea and possibly the first American troops to face the enemy after Bataan.

A black aviation engineer battalion participated in the victory of the Battle of the Coral Sea in 1942 and worked twenty-four hours a day to build an airdrome in New Caledonia. In April, 1944, the Ninety-third Infantry Division had its

A popular postwar film was ***Home of the Brave*** with actor James Edwards.

Singer Nat "King" Cole and his trio rose to prominence in the forties.

Top black singers during postwar years were (l.-r.) Sarah Vaughan, Billy Eckstine and Dinah Washington.

first action at Empress Augusta Bay on Bougainville Island in the Solomons. By the end of the month, the Ninety-third had secured the Saua River and a portion of the land east of the Torokina River, and went on to the Treasury Island group, and to Morotai Island in the Dutch East Indies and the Philippines.

Many blacks received citations for brave and meritorious service. The main parade ground of the armored forces at Fort Knox, Kentucky, was named Brooks Field in memory of Private Robert H.

Brooks, son of a Kentucky sharecropper who was the first American soldier of the armored force killed in the Pacific. One of the outstanding heroes of the Coast Guard was Charles V. David Jr., a mess attendant who gave his life rescuing his executive officer from the waters of the Atlantic during rescue operations of a torpedoed transport. David's widow was awarded the Navy and Marine Corps Medal, one of the highest naval awards.

Among the winged heroes of the war was Captain Leonard M. Jackson, of Fort Worth, Texas, who received the Distinguished Flying Cross and the Air Medal with seven clusters for destroying three German planes. A member of the Ninety-ninth Fighter Squadron, Captain Jackson flew 142 missions. Colonel Benjamin Davis Jr., Washington, D.C., won the Distinguished Flying Cross, the Silver Star, the Legion of Merit, and the Air Medal with four Oak Leaf Clusters for courage and combat ability. George Watson, a private in the Quartermaster Corps, from Birmingham, Alabama, was the first black man to win the Distinguished Service Cross for extraordinary heroism in World War II. The award was granted posthumously for bravery shown at Pordoch Harbor, New Guinea, in assisting

Coleman Hawkins was a major jazz figure of the thirties and forties.

Jazz composer Duke Ellington consults with long-time associate and arranger Billy Strayhorn

several men to a raft from their sinking boat. Overcome by exhaustion, he was pulled under by the suction of the craft and drowned.

A partial list of 273 army awards—omitting the Purple Heart given to those wounded in action—granted to black personnel was released in October, 1945. The list included three Distinguished Service Crosses for "extraordinary heroism . . . against an army enemy"; one Distinguished Service Medal for "exceptionally meritorious service to the government in a duty of great responsibility"; the Legion of Merit to twelve blacks for "exceptionally meritorious conduct in the performance of outstanding services"; seventeen Silver Stars for "gallantry in action in orders"; sixty-eight Soldier's Medals; 164 Bronze Star Medals and four Air Medals. In addition, three blacks, excluding Miller, received the Navy Cross. By war's end, the number of Distinguished Flying Crosses had increased to seventy-nine. The Distinguished Service Medal was awarded Campbell C. Johnson, colonel and executive assistant to the director of Selective Service in Washington, D.C. The Distinguished Civilian Service Award was granted to Lester B. Granger, special adviser to the secretary of the navy, New York; and the Medal for Merit for Civilians was given to Truman K. Gib-

Black dancers Pearl Primus (above) and Katherine Dunham, whose dance company won international fame.

The school of modern jazz rose to prominence through the music of saxophonist Charlie Parker and trumpeter Miles Davis (l.).

A leader in the "bebop" music era was trumpet player Dizzy Gillespie.

son, Jr., civilian aide to the secretary of war, Chicago.

Despite the ultimate achievements of blacks in the war, the struggle to gain equality for blacks in industry and the armed services had created attitudes of apprehension and bitterness among blacks on the home front. For the most part, blacks remained economically and educationally deprived. In 1941, Dr. Guy B. Johnson made this observation in the *Annals of the American Academy of Political and Social Science:* "On any scale of economic adequacy or inadequacy—measured, e.g., in terms of number employed, number on relief, number in unskilled occupations, number in professional work, income levels—the Negro would have to be rated as from two to four times worse off than the white man."

Southern black workers poured into Northern cities during the war years to work in defense industries, and housing became a major problem. Bombings and riots resulted as whites objected violently to "invading" blacks. There were also serious riots at Southern training centers. Jim Crow signs were common in the South. There were "white" and "colored" benches in parks, "white" and "colored" water fountains and separate entrances to theaters, stores, and even separate pay windows in industrial plants.

In 1942 and 1943, A. Philip Randolph had succeeded in creating the first American nonviolent movement and the first black mass movement that was not based on black nationalism. His March on Washington movement was an organized campaign against discrimination and segregation and had branches in both North and South in the summer of 1942. Randolph was called the "American Gandhi" for his proposals for an all-out nonviolent assault on American racism. He proposed school, streetcar, and bus boycotts, marches on city halls, and the White House "until the country and the

Ralph Bunche became acting mediator during the 1949 Palestine crisis. He had served as chief aide to Count Folke Bernadotte (below, center), who was later assassinated.

world recognizes the Negro has become of age and will sacrifice his all to be counted as men, free men."

The NAACP and its executive secretary Walter White also emerged as formidable forces during the war years. NAACP membership rose sharply from sixty-five thousand in 1940 to five hundred thousand in 1945. Black individuals like pacifist Bayard Rustin, Lewis Jones, and Elijah Muhammed and some of his Muslim followers, served prison sentences as conscientious objectors and refused to fight in a segregated army for a segregated country.

The black press became a formidable foe of segregation as blacks received a new image and sense of pride in the columns of new magazines like *Negro Digest*, published by John H. Johnson. Johnson followed with *Ebony*, a monthly picture magazine and *Jet*, a weekly. Other magazines that developed during this period were *Our World* and *Headlines* and *Pictures*. These magazines played significant roles in the new posture that blacks would assume.

White backlash, reached panic proportions in the South. Some white journalists and businessmen, incensed by the anti-discrimination legislation and rising black protest, said that if winning the war meant black equality, they preferred to lose the war.

The summer of 1943, which was marred by riots, marked a turning point in black-white relations.

The riots began in February, 1942, at the Sojourner Truth Housing Projects in Detroit. When the first black families attempted to move into the project on February 28, a band of white pickets approached them with clubs and bats. The police were called, and, in a short time, a truckload of blacks, also armed with clubs, arrived on the scene. The ensuing battle turned into a free-for-all as police joined the whites in battling the blacks. It was some time before the disturbance could be quelled, and it was not until several weeks later that the blacks were permitted to move into the projects.

In the spring of 1943, during a critical production shortage, a reconstituted President's Committee on Fair Employment Practices forced the Union of Marine

Bunche receives the Nobel Peace Prize in Oslo, Norway for his efforts as mediator. He later became a UN Deputy Secretary General.

Private First Class William Thompson (l.) was posthumously awarded the Congressional Medal of Honor for valor in Korea, the first black man to be so honored since the Spanish-American War. Sergeant Cornelius H. Charlton also received the Medal of Honor during the Korean War.

Shipbuilders and the Alabama Drydock and Shipbuilding Company to promote a small group of blacks to vacancies as welders in a Mobile, Alabama, shipyard. As soon as news of the promotions got around, a mob of white workers surrounded the blacks and began beating them. The battle continued for several hours, during which time several blacks were severely injured. All blacks were ordered from the yard until the dispute could be settled. Government officials decided later to provide a segregated shipyard where blacks could advance to highly skilled positions.

Beaumont, Texas, was a war industrial center with a large number of blacks restricted to unskilled jobs. On June 9, 1943, a white woman claimed that she had been raped by a black man she had hired to cut her lawn. Several suspects were arrested, but the woman could not identify her alleged assailant. The woman's three children even claimed that they had not seen a man around the house. Soon after the woman's charges became known, a rumor circulated that a black suspect had been arrested. A mob of white men appeared at the jail and demanded the man. When they found no such suspect, the angered white mob went to the black business section of the city and engaged in an orgy of violence and vandalism that lasted for several hours. Texas Rangers were ordered into the area and martial law was declared. More than seventy-five blacks were injured—two fatally—and several hundred thousand dollars worth of property was destroyed.

The Los Angeles "Zoot Suit" riot occurred during the weekend of June 3, 1943. It was rumored in the area that teenaged boys wearing zoot suits were attacking servicemen. On the evening of June 3 a group of Mexican youths, members of the Alpine Club, were assaulted by a mob of servicemen. Until June 7 mobs of white servicemen—sometimes numbering thousands—roamed freely through Mexican and black neighborhoods assaulting anyone they found wearing a "zoot suit."

By far the bloodiest and most destructive riot of the war years was the huge Detroit riot of June 20, 1943, in which thirty-four persons were killed and more than 461 injured. Over a million man-hours were lost in war production, resulting in a significant reduction in factory operations. Looting and vandalism resulted in losses exceeding $2,000,000 and the federal government spent at least $100,000 per day on soldiers who were sent to the area.

The precipitating incidents of the Detroit riot occurred in crowded Belle Isle Recreational Park. In the course of several confrontations between blacks and whites, a rumor started that a white man had thrown a black woman and her baby from Belle Isle Bridge into the river. Among whites there was a story that a black man had shot a white woman on the bridge. Other rumors, and enlargement of these rumors, passed along quickly until a group of white sailors stationed them-

An integrated American artillery crew fires in support of an assault on Triangle Hill in Korea.

Captain Daniel (Chappie) James (l.) was one of many blacks to serve in integrated units during the Korean War period.

selves on the road leading from the bridge and began a systematic attack on blacks returning to the city. White civilians soon joined in the attacks, while white police stood idly by. In a black neighborhood, a public address system in a black dance hall was used to announce the rumored incident of the black mother and her baby. In the two days of heavy rioting which followed, mobs of whites roamed Woodward Avenue beating and stoning blacks and upsetting their autos. At the same time mobs of blacks roamed through Paradise Valley beating white persons, upsetting their autos and looting white businesses. After several false starts, Detroit's mayor called in federal troops.

Six weeks later Harlem erupted into rioting when, on August 1, 1943, James Collins, a policeman on duty in a Harlem hotel, attempted to arrest a young black women for disorderly conduct. A black military policeman, Robert Bandy, was alleged to have interfered with the arrest and to have struck the policeman with his own nightstick. The policeman allegedly shot Bandy, wounding him slightly. Both were hospitalized. A crowd followed the wounded men to the hospital and milled around exchanging various rumors. In a few hours, the crowd had grown to three thousand. Someone threw bottles from a roof and the crowd dispersed, regrouped and surged up the main streets of Harlem, smashing shop windows and looting as they went. Fifty-three white policemen were assaulted.

Coupled with the return of the considerably enlightened black veteran to American society was the emerging leadership in Africa and Asia. Partly because of the war, African nations pressed the question of colonialism and called for self-government. These stirrings of African nationalism that culminated in self-determination for most of black Africa were influenced significantly by Marcus Garvey and his Universal Negro Improvement Association of the 1920's and by the Pan-African movement of W. E. B. Du Bois.

The formation of the United Nations in 1945 as a world peace-making body created a new arena of protest for black Americans, Africans, and Asians. The world's black and yellow people had been virtually ignored by the old League of Nations. When fascist Italy's air force strafed and bombed defenseless Ethiopia in 1936, Emperor Haile Selassie's appeal for League of Nations intervention had fallen on deaf ears. But with Africa's new insistence on self-government, the Afro-Asian members of the UN became a powerful bloc.

When the UN first met in 1946, only two of its fifty-one charter members, Ethiopia and Liberia, represented African nations. There were also seven Middle-Eastern members as well as three Asian countries. By 1965, the number of Africans in the UN had risen to thirty-five out of a total of 115 nations.

In 1948, Ralph Bunche was named acting UN mediator in the 1948 Palestine dispute. In 1950, Dr. Bunche received the Nobel Peace Prize for his work in this crisis. Later he became UN deputy secretary-general in charge of political affairs.

Black and white troops participate in a training exercise at Grafenwohr, Germany.

An activist during the war and postwar years was brilliant black strategist W. E. B. Du Bois, shown here in the New York City office of the NAACP. Staffers included (l.-r.) national director Walter White, Thurgood Marshall, Henry Moon, Lucille Black, and Roy Wilkins.

During this same period, the civil rights struggle moved to a new level. Some blacks and black organizations, in search of ways to relieve discrimination and segregation, allied themselves with the Progressive party, which openly attacked the existing parties and gave blacks many positions of real power within party ranks. More than thirty blacks ran for state and federal offices on the 1948 party ticket. Henry Wallace, the party's presidential candidate, campaigned in the South with an integrated staff. In several states white mobs attempted to break up the meetings.

With the severance of American and Russian relations during the Cold War, the Progressive ideology and most forms of black revolt fell into disfavor. Black organizations began barring radicals from their ranks. Picketing and mass demonstrations became "dangerous" forms of dissent. Militant black leadership virtually disappeared.

Another interesting development was the organization of the Congress of Racial Equality (CORE), which was formed in Chicago in 1942. CORE staged its first "sit-in" in a restaurant in the Windy City's Loop. The organization succeeded in desegregating the restaurant and moved on to other sit-ins in St. Louis and Baltimore.

At the end of the war there was no change in the army's attitudes toward segregation. President Truman issued Executive Order 9808 in 1946, which created a Presidential Committee on Civil Rights to study existing federal protection

Lester Granger, executive secretary of the National Urban League, was special adviser to the secretary of the navy during World War II.

of civil rights and ways to improve it. Blacks on the Committee included Attorney Sadie T. Alexander and Dr. Channing Tobias, director of the Phelps-Stokes Fund.

In October, 1947, A. Philip Randolph and the Reverend Grant Reynolds formed a Committee against Jim Crow in Military Service and Training. Shortly after Randolph and Reynolds received a promise from the Democratic National Committee that a statement against a segregated draft act would be issued, but no action was taken. On March 22, 1948, Randolph and other concerned citizens met with the president and requested his support for antisegregation amendments to the proposed draft bill. Again, nothing was done and in June of 1948, Randolph formed the League for Non-Violent Civil Disobedience Against Military Segregation. He threatened to urge blacks to resist induction by civil disobedience unless segregation and discrimination in the armed forces were banned. Responding to Randolph's political strength, Truman issued Executive Order 9981 in July, barring segregation in the armed forces, and created the President's Committee on Equality of Treatment and Opportunity in the Armed Services. Blacks on the Committee were Lester Granger, executive secretary of the Urban League, and John Sengstacke, editor of the *Chicago Defender*. This committee later became known as the Fahy Committee. In May, 1950, the committee issued a report *Freedom to Serve,* which called for equality of opportunity in the armed services. Unfortunately, the Fahy Committee substantially affected only the navy. The entry of America into the Korean War one month later and an immediate need for troops was responsible for desegregation in the army.

Another notable postwar event was the 1947 NAACP petition to the UN outlining in detail a factual history of the denial of human rights and appealing to the UN for a redress of grievances. W. E. B. Du Bois was among the scholars who worked on the document; and while it brought no concrete results, it did add the weight of world opinion to the domestic pressure against segregation. Paul Robeson presented another appeal to the UN on behalf of the Civil Rights Congress. Robeson's report charged the United States with racial genocide.

A race riot in Athens, Alabama, in 1946 was touched off by a fistfight between two white veterans and a black man. A white mob of about two thousand knocked down and trampled blacks, injuring between fifty and one hundred. Ten whites were arrested, including the two involved in the fistfight. A local state guard company was mobilized and police from northern Alabama were called to restore order.

When a black bus driver, Harvey E. Clark, a veteran, tried to move into a Cicero, Illinois, apartment building in 1951, his windows were smashed and his furniture was thrown out of the windows and burned. A mob of about 3,500 gathered and rioted until about 450 National Guardsmen and about two hundred Cicero and Cook County police put down the disorder. An announcement was later

Black veteran Harvey Clark, was ousted from a "white" apartment building in Cicero, Illinois, which was later integrated.

made by the NAACP that the building had been bought by blacks and would house both black and white veterans.

Lynchings also increased significantly. In 1946, six blacks were lynched. Between 1947 and 1962, twelve blacks were lynched. In 1955 a fourteen-year-old Chicagoan, Emmett Till, while visiting relatives in Money, Mississippi, allegedly whistled at a white woman. A mob of whites kidnapped the youth and lynched him. The case was highly publicized, even

A black family seeking residence in Trumbull Park Housing Project in Chicago, faced a rock-throwing white mob in 1953. Police maintained a twenty-four hour vigil.

A major figure in NAACP legal fights in the forties and fifties, Ada Lois Sipuel sought entry to the University of Oklahoma.

G.W. McLaurin asked the courts to order the University of Oklahoma to admit black students.

abroad. The lynchers were, however, cleared of all charges.

Education, housing, and interstate travel were major areas of concern for blacks in the post-war years. During the war, there had been a series of school strikes. The opening of the school year in 1945 saw major demonstrations in integrated schools as whites protested the enrollment of black students. The major school strikes were in Gary, Indiana, New York City, Chicago, and San Diego.

When Ada Lois Sipuel was denied admission to the University of Oklahoma in 1946, the NAACP won a Supreme Court decision which said: "A state must offer schooling for Negroes as soon as it pro-

The University admitted McLaurin but segregated him in a special section outside the classroom.

vides for whites." Within two months, the same court ruled in *Shelley* vs. *Kraemer* that federal and state courts could not enforce "restrictive covenants" in housing. Two years later, the Supreme Court took another significant step in the companion test cases of *Sweatt* vs. *Painter* and *McLaurin* vs. *Oklahoma*. Herman Sweatt, a graduate of allblack Wiley College in Marshall, Texas, and a graduate student at the University of Michigan, applied for admission to the law school at the University of Texas in 1946 and was denied admission. University of Texas President T. S. Painter immediately sought a ruling from the state attorney general who ruled in Painter's favor. A federal district court and the Supreme Court overruled that decision. The McLaurin case was a test of the legality of discrimination and segregation in the field of higher education. A black student had challenged the right of the University of Oklahoma to put blacks in segregated seating and eating facilities. Again the Supreme Court ruled that such a practice promoted inequality in education. These decisions set the stage for the significant case of *Brown* vs. *Board of Edu-*

The Supreme Court hearings on school desegregation, initiated by the NAACP, were attended by spectators from all over the nation. A group of Howard University students wait in line to attend the hearing.

Members of the NAACP legal team discuss pending hearings in the Supreme Court Bar Room. Left to right are Elwood Chisolm, Oliver Hill, Thurgood Marshall, Spottswood Robinson, Harold Boulware, and Jack Greenberg.

cation of 1954. This case reversed the *Plessy* decision of 1896. Brown's case involved a Kansas statute requiring segregated classrooms in both elementary and high schools. "Slavery is perpetuated in these statutes," Thurgood Marshall insisted and the court ruled in his favor. The court said: "We cannot turn the clock back to 1868 when the Amendment was adopted, or even to 1896 when *Plessy* vs. *Ferguson* was written. We must consider public education in the light of its full development and its present place in American life throughout the Nation. . . . We conclude that in the field of public education, the doctrine of 'separate but equal' has no place." This decision would set the stage for the most massive assault on segregated schooling in the history of America.

A unanimous court decision, in 1955, ordered desegregation "with all deliberate speed." Voluntary integration took place in several Border States but the Deep South resisted.

Ku Klux Klan membership rose and White Citizens councils were formed. Racial violence increased; and in one year there were 530 killings, bombings, and beatings. Black teachers affiliated with the NAACP were fired or threatened, and tensions in the South reached a fever pitch.

It was against this background, and in a climate of deepening crisis, that black America moved from the portentous postwar years to a new era of unprecedented public protest.

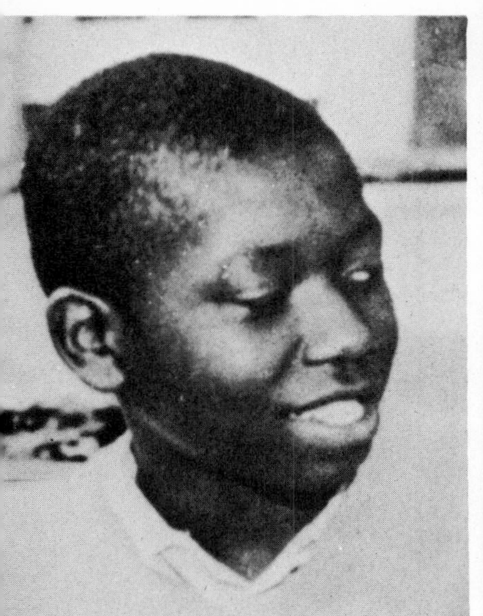

A successful NAACP desegregation suit involved Spottswood Thomas Bolling (l.) and NAACP attorneys (l.-r.) George E. C. Hayes, Thurgood Marshall, chief legal counsel, and James Nabrit Jr.

A summit meeting of black Southern leaders was held in Atlanta in 1955 to formulate plans for implementation of the Supreme Court ruling on school desegregation.